PEACE
TO THE
PIECES

HOW TO RECOVER FROM TRAUMA

Crowned Image Ministries, Inc.
Thompson's Station, TN 37179

Printed in the U.S.A.

ISBN: 978-1-946622-17-4

For more information:
crownedimage.com

PEACE
TO THE
PIECES
HOW TO RECOVER FROM TRAUMA

RACHEL CORDERO

&

AMBER WRIGHT

To Jennifer and Munday Martin and Contagious Love International.
Without you, this book could not have materialized in the manner it has.
Thank you for trusting us and allowing us to partner with your hearts.

To our steadfast husbands, children, parents, family, and friends;
your prayers and support have been a life raft that continues to carry us.
Thank you for sharing us and always welcoming us home with warm hugs.

We love you all dearly.

CONTENTS

Foreword

Introduction

One: Permission   1

Two: Trauma   7

Three: Your Brain   15

Four: Stress   25

Five: Triggers   33

Six: Demons   39

Seven: Silent Killers   47

Eight: Comfort   57

Nine: Healing   71

Ten: Calming   81

Eleven: Connecting   87

Twelve: Communicating   93

Thirteen: Rescue   103

Fourteen: PTKW   113

Fifteen: Perspective   117

Afterword   125

FOREWORD

Peace to the Pieces has been the missing piece to deliverance ministry that the world desperately needs.

Rachel and Amber take your hands—one on your left side and one on your right—and walk with you one step at a time until your heart begins to mend.

I personally can attest to watching them take people on a journey from their past hurts right through the present pain, giving them understanding of why they are hurting and clarity on what it takes to heal.

Healing is possible. Rachel and Amber teach us that through gentle words filled with deep compassion and love. I know their hearts. They have a burden to see your heart fly free. I've watched them weep over a person for a long time, wanting so badly for their freedom to come. And it does. Little by little, layer by layer. The fire of God's love pouring from them melts the waxy coat of pain off any broken heart.

There is such a thing as true love. It comes from God, and His desire is for it to so fill our hearts that everything else burns away in its heat. This love abides within the spirits of Rachel and Amber. They will not rest until every heart knows that it is loved.

There is a place called freedom. There is a place called accepted. There is a place called Peace.

I believe you will see it by the end of these pages. I pray that your pieces will finally come to rest. Let Rachel and Amber take you to that place with the turn of every page.

Welcome home, friend.

- Jennifer Martin
Co-Founder
Contagious Love International

INTRODUCTION

Hi, Friend.

It's a brave thing to pick up a book on trauma. Braver still to actually read it, let alone engage with its contents. These are already steps you have made toward healing; well done. No, seriously, well done.

Our heart with this resource is to help you understand where you may have been impacted by trauma throughout your life and not fully recognize its presence or the extent of its reach. That's not all. There are so many resources available to define, examine, and study the impact of trauma— plenty of good resources. The gap we have seen, however, is in the availability of answers about how to navigate healing after discovery, how to recover, where to find hope, and where to take all the questions that trauma can stir within us. This is our greater goal. Hope. Healing. Freedom. Wholeness.

We want you to know that we understand the tender nature of this topic. Trauma is painful. Facing our pain takes incredible courage. Our hearts are for you and with you. We have prayed fervently for the Lord to be so close to you as you read these words, as you journey with Him, and as you open your heart once again to the hope that there is more healing for you.

The Holy Spirit will be with you if you desire Him to be, if you invite Him. He longs to be your Comforter and Healer. This resource was His idea; your freedom is His idea; your healing is His idea – He wants it even more than you do.

"Yet when the holy lovers of God cry out to him with all their hearts, the Lord will hear them and come to rescue them from all their troubles. The Lord is close to all whose hearts are crushed by pain, and He is always ready to restore the repentant one. Even when bad things happen to the good and godly ones, the Lord will save them and not let them be defeated by what they face" (Psalm 34:17-19 TPT).

Take His hand, take our hands, let us journey together. You are not alone in these pages, Dear One.

CHAPTER ONE

PERMISSION

If we asked you to close your eyes and try to recall your earliest memory, what would it be? Honestly, take a moment. Center your thoughts. Still your mind. Breathe, and ask Holy Spirit to bring to your remembrance your earliest memory. Take your time.

What did you recall?

Were you younger than five? Older than five?
Was it a happy memory? A fearful one?
Was it a lot of information or a snippet of a moment?

Did you know that our earliest memory with imagery attached to it is most often the first time our brain registered a significant shift in our worldview?

It could have been something like the first time you experienced snow. Playing outside with friends. The first time a significant injury was experienced. A trip to the dentist. So many things can impact your worldview.

My (Rachel's) earliest memory was the morning of my fifth birthday. I was sitting in a chair in the kitchen, tying the shoelaces (a newly acquired skill I was excited about) on my red sneakers as I was getting ready to ride the bus with my sister to preschool. I looked up at my biological mother (I was later adopted), who was combing my sister's hair, and asked her if we could have "pahsghetti" (my attempt at the word spaghetti) for dinner that night since it was my birthday. She quickly reminded me that we didn't celebrate birthdays because our church at the time believed it was vanity.

My worldview was shaping. That day's education taught me it is vain to be celebrated, and God dislikes vanity.

I (Amber) can still see my first memory in vivid detail. It was the day fear was conceived inside of me with the intent to destroy. At the tender age of two years old, I remember seeing, with my natural eyes, a demon standing at the top of the stairs that led down to our basement. It was a tall, black, shadowy figure. I remember how fast my hands covered my ears as a high-pitched sound pierced my head. My worldview was very quickly formed at that moment, teaching me that living shadows dwell in basements, and they aren't kind at all. They are scary. I knew this figure wanted to harm me, and it was the first time I remember being afraid.

What about you, friend? What shaped your worldview? Was it something pleasant or something fearful? Where has the collection of memories, experiences, and perceptions about life brought you as an adult?

We all know that people are unique. Even down to our fingerprints, we are incredibly unique. No two human beings in all of creation, in all of history, have ever been exactly the same. True? Absolutely. Did you know that our view of the world around us is as unique as our fingerprints? Identical twins growing up in the same household, doing the same things every day of their childhood, would still have two distinct worldviews. The way you perceive life is as unique as your DNA.

Your life experiences are incomparable. They do not require definition or qualification by anyone else. The way your heart, mind, body, and spirit experience life are unique to you. This includes events that may have registered to your mind and soul as traumatic.

In the coming pages, we will talk further about worldview, how our brains develop, and the impact trauma can have on our developing minds. But for now, we want to encourage you and validate the understanding that you are fearfully, wonderfully, and uniquely created by God. Your experiences are valid. Your history matters. Your wounds are important to the heart of the Lord.

You have permission to heal. You have permission to understand. You have permission to be whole.

There is no shame here. You do not have to silence the needs of your soul. You have permission to understand why you feel the way you do, why you hurt the way you do. You have permission to understand the reason why you react the way you do or think the way you do.

The Bible says in Proverbs 4:7, *"Wisdom is the principal thing; therefore, get wisdom. And in all of your getting, get understanding."*

You have permission to unpack. To not have to have it all together. To know you aren't disappointing God and failing as a believer when your heart is broken. A broken heart or a wounded soul is not the consequence of a lack of faith. So many people have been smacked in the face with these harsh words in moments when their heart was the most tender, "Well, if you just believed where the Scriptures say…fill in the blank… you wouldn't feel that way!" God's Word was never meant to be used as an assault weapon. We apologize to you on behalf of every person who ever mishandled His heart and His words and used them as a weapon against you.

There is a reason you feel the way you do. There is a cause to what makes you anxious, or fearful, or depressed, or shut down, or over-attached to others, or under-attached to others. You weren't born with a broken heart. There is wisdom in searching out the why behind your thoughts and feelings.

Can we encourage you not to silence the voice of your heart and your soul?

Even when our emotions tell us things that may not line up with reality, there is something to discern. Our emotions do not lead us, but we can examine our emotions and discover much about our internal processing. This is a valid and often overlooked process, a process which leads us to ask,

"Why?" Why are we thinking what we are thinking? Why are we feeling what we are feeling? So often, we judge and shut down the emotion without digging to the root to discover why it is there in the first place.

So much of the sin and brokenness in our lives is born this way. When we shame our feelings or shut down our thoughts and emotions without examining them, we also tend to ignore legitimate human needs. When you ignore legitimate needs, the world, the flesh, and the devil are quick to offer illegitimate solutions. If you shut down the need for love or comfort, the Enemy is quick to provide false comforts that lead to deeply rooted sin patterns of bondage.

We travel with a ministry group that leads events all over the country. City after city, state after state, we encounter a similar theme among God's people: overlooked legitimate needs.

I (Rachel) remember one night in particular when we were ministering in a small gathering in a small town. The evening had been so sweetly filled with the precious presence of the Holy Spirit. We had worshiped, heard a compelling word from the heart of the Lord, and had been praying for people for a couple of hours at that point. I noticed this gentleman, probably in his late sixties, had been standing nearby, waiting for me. I finished with the person I had been praying for and turned towards him. His wife quickly came up behind him; they were both in tears. I looked at his face; his gentle blue eyes looked lost, like a scared little boy. Tears streamed down his face, and his voice quivered as he choked out a confession.

"I've been addicted to pornography for nearly forty years...."

That was all he could get out before he broke and began to sob. His wife began to speak for him and shared briefly that this had been something they had fought against but felt defeated by for their entire marriage. Yet here she was, right by his side; they were contending for freedom still.

In a flash before me, I saw the Holy Spirit giving a glimpse of what this man looked like as an eight-year-old boy. Tender. Afraid. Longing for comfort and finding none. As if in one glimpse, the Holy Spirit offered the entire backstory of WHY this man had struggled for so long. He longed for comfort and didn't know how to access it. I saw pictures in my mind's eye of him reaching out to his mother for comfort and not finding it. That's when the Enemy offered him a way to comfort himself.

Is this the root for every person who struggles with pornography? I'm not saying that. But this is what the Holy Spirit revealed about this particular man in this specific moment because I wasn't assuming why he was in this place or how he got here. There was a pause. A question was asked of the One who knows all. There was first a moment of understanding before judging the circumstance and declaring a formula and prescription.

I quietly leaned forward and shared the pictures I saw with this sweet gentleman and asked him if any of it made sense to him. He began to weep from an even deeper place than shame and desperation; he began to weep from a place of understanding. I could hear the Holy Spirit wanting me to encourage him that his needs for comfort are legitimate and valid, needs that are meant to be fulfilled by God Himself in all the creative ways that God meets our needs.

We prayed together. Shame lifted off of him. Addiction lifted off of him. So much quiet deliverance happened in those moments, and the God of all peace came in and washed over him with the very thing his unsatisfied soul had been longing to experience for more than forty years – comfort.

The key is pausing to understand.

Will you pause to understand? Will you choose not to shame your own heart and your own needs and to stop for a moment to understand? You are worth pausing for. You are worth the time it takes to discover the "why" behind the struggles you are facing.

Do you know one of the most undervalued aspects of loving people is in the form of listening? Being heard makes us feel loved. There is so much noise in the world and so many opinions; we are inundated with information and bombarded with words and content. When was the last time you felt heard and understood? When someone stops talking and listens, really listens, engages with empathy and the desire to understand, doesn't that make you feel loved? Think about it. When was the last time someone listened to you, validated you, and DID NOT follow up by talking about themselves or relating your situation to a story about them? This is a potent kind of love, to listen to others, to actually hear them, to let the whole thing be about what they need without having to talk or relate it back to ourselves.

The Holy Spirit wants to do this with you. He wants to listen and help you understand your own heart. He wants to help you pause, wait, and seek to understand. He will help you gain revelation about yourself. He will listen and minister to your heart, if you will let Him. If you will pause for yourself and take the time to be patient and understanding with yourself, He will provide the revelation and the comfort.

Just think, you allowing God to love you in this way will enable Him to also deposit love into you that will come into full bloom and overflow into how you love others as well. You will get free and become a person who listens with love and offers understanding to others.

So, posture your heart, Dear One. In patience. In seeking to understand. In receiving God's love. Posture your heart to be listened to and understood. Posture your heart to receive healing. Healing is just ahead.

CHAPTER TWO

TRAUMA

What images come to your mind when you read or hear the word trauma?

Do you hear the words Post Traumatic Stress Disorder or PTSD, complex trauma, battle fatigue, or shell shock syndrome? Does it make you think of war veterans or severe cases of sexual assault?

Does it make your own heart race a little or make it slightly harder to breathe?

For many years the vast scope of trauma's impact went widely unrecognized. Effects of trauma were undetected or written off as character issues, personality traits, or behavioral problems. While medications to treat the symptoms of trauma became increasingly available, the understanding of the root cause of the symptoms did not. Really it has only been within the last two decades that the extent of trauma's impact is becoming more widely investigated. Even still, the medical and research communities are hard-pressed to agree on even a definition of trauma.

Look at the culture around us, though. Look at the number of people bound by depression, anxiety, and confusion. It is not hard to see the brokenness in the world around us. It is not hard to see the lonely and the lost. It is not hard to see the isolation and defeat. What might surprise you, however, is how much of these factors can actually be traced back to a root of trauma.

Trauma is not just a condition to describe the heartbreaking consequences felt by our precious men and women in the armed forces when they have been subjected to life on the front lines. It is much more widespread than that.

Trauma is the lasting effect on a person's mind, body, soul, and emotions as a result of living through a deeply distressing event or events.

A deeply distressing event doesn't take an act of war; it only requires a deeply distressing event.

Every deeply distressing event has the potential to shift our worldview. It impacts and changes the way we perceive ourselves and the world around us. What once felt safe may not feel safe anymore. After a singular trauma-causing event, a person's entire perception of himself or herself can shift. Even the way we relate to others can suddenly change after trauma has been experienced.

Sometimes our sense of identity and safety, as well as our relating patterns, were built upon a foundation laid by trauma in the first place; and we have been responding from a traumatized place all along without even realizing it. What if the fears or anxieties you experience regularly don't stem from personality or perceived weakness but from a root of trauma? The presence of trauma in our lives genuinely limits our ability to achieve a sense of peace and calm. Not to mention that it also often carries with it a deep sense of shame, helplessness, and torment.

Where do we find the line between a distressing event and a deeply distressing, trauma-inducing event? How do I know if I have experienced trauma or not?

It is essential to know that what causes trauma to one person may not cause trauma to another person. I (Rachel) grew up in a house with four biological sisters. We each have our own worldview, and we each have different things that registered to us as trauma that may not have impacted our other siblings the same way. This is true of everyone. What impacts one person in a traumatic way may not affect someone else who is even experiencing the same situation in the same way.

Whether or not an event is considered one of trauma depends on how quickly the person in the experience can return to whatever his or her standard of normal may be. Stress in life is inescapable. It is needed for our development, which we will discuss more in-depth later. But the difference between a stressful event, or even a distressing event, and one that is so deeply distressing that it causes a traumatic impact to the person experiencing it, is dependent upon how long it takes to return to a place of normalcy.

Let's consider this situation. Several years ago, when I (Rachel) was dating the man who would become my husband, we were driving back from church on Easter Sunday when we came upon a car accident that had just happened. A young girl had been texting and driving when she lost control of her vehicle. It crossed over the greenway in the middle of the highway and hit a family in an SUV, causing their vehicle to roll several times before landing on its side. The young girl was unconscious in the front seat of her car and had several other drivers of the stopped traffic coming to her aid and calling the paramedics. The other vehicle was on its side, the driver's window facing up, and the family was trapped inside.

My boyfriend at the time (and let me mention that this was a moment that sealed in my heart that I would absolutely marry him if he asked me) parked our car and headed across the road to help the family. He climbed up on the side of the car and pulled the entire family out of the vehicle through the broken driver's side window, which was very timely because the vehicle was leaking gas everywhere. This included pulling the father, the mother, and their toddler, who had been stuck in her car seat, unable to get out, through the top of the wedged car to safety.

Would you consider this to be a distressing event?

Well, let's examine that because there are several different characters at play in this scenario. My now husband was not at all impacted by the stress of the event. He loves to help, and being called upon for such heroics was invigorating to him. His body experienced stress at the moment, but he didn't experience any compromised ability to return to his normal level of calm after the situation subsided. The parents in the SUV experienced a level of stress that would indicate it had been a distressing event for them. Still, they were able to return to their standard of normalcy and calm within several weeks. The young girl who was driving had an impact of trauma because her heart races still anytime someone is driving and looks at their phone for even a moment. The baby girl who was trapped in the car seat experienced a traumatic event because, for months, she cried every time she heard the car seat belt click into place, and she was agitated in general any time she was in the car.

All these people experienced the same event; only some experienced it as trauma, while others did not. The difference was each person's level of resiliency and ability to return to their normal state of calmness after the event.

What kind of events can cause trauma?

Once we have expanded our understanding to realize that trauma is not reserved only as a condition for those who have endured extreme experiences such as war veterans, being a witness to a murder, or a victim of child abuse (though these are profoundly distressing and valid experiences to feel understandably impacted by), we have to consider all kinds of distressing situations and realize trauma may be present.

Trauma can come from any kind of violation. Trauma can be present with any abuse, neglect, or the very often overlooked condition of simply not being loved well. Trauma can take root in any form of bullying or even humiliation. How many reports of teenage suicide are linked to peer bullying?

We want to help you understand this because trauma is so often misunderstood, misdiagnosed, or glossed over.

It is helpful to mention also that it isn't that a single episode of loss or that every deeply distressing event will cause trauma, but even a single episode of distress can cause trauma. This depends on the depth of the event and the level of support and resiliency of the individual who is experiencing it.

Remember that resiliency is the ability to come back to a personal standard of normal after an event is experienced.

I (Amber) can give you an example of a trauma that I experienced related to being humiliated. When I was in third grade, I had a very mean teacher. She did not like me for some reason, and I was never clear on why. She would walk by my desk and pinch me or push my head down into the desk on whatever I was working on. She was just cruel. It made going to school feel like torture, and I loved school! I was not a particularly ornery child by any means. I preferred to be pleasing and follow the rules; I am still this way. So, I still don't understand why she was so hateful to me.

One day she told me to come up in front of the class. As I stood there, she promptly told the whole class, "Say goodbye to Amber, everyone. She won't be returning to class any longer as she is going to be moved to the retarded class!" Heat flooded through my face, my heart began to race as my breathing shallowed, and my palms began to sweat.

She told me I was leaving with this man waiting in the hallway to take a "retarded test." Yes, that is what they called it when I was in third grade. Much to my humiliation, as I turned to look towards the door at who she was talking about, one of the children in the class started to chant, "Retard! Retard! Amber is a retard!" Before I got to the door, the entire class had joined in unison, "Retard! Retard! Amber is a retard!"

Interestingly, I obediently followed that gentleman into this tiny little room and took the test they requested, followed by another test and another. Only to have it determined that I was actually meant to be in the "gifted" class. Before I returned to class, the gentleman who had administered the test asked my teacher to join us in the hallway. There he sternly reprimanded her for the accusations she made about my learning capacities and instructed her to send me to the gifted class in the afternoons from there on out.

Such a quick redemption should have restored the damage done to my heart earlier that day, shouldn't it? It didn't. For decades, my palms would sweat, my heart raced, and heat would flush over my face every time I was in a position of standing in front of a group of people. I had been impacted by a traumatizing experience.

Trauma can also come from a consistent absence or lack of something that should be happening. You were created to be loved. You were knit together in your mother's womb, dreamed up in the heart of a loving Creator, and breathed into existence by His love.

Ephesians 3:17–19 says, *"That Christ may dwell in your hearts through faith; that you, being rooted and grounded in love, may be able to comprehend with all the saints what is the width and length and depth and height—to know the love of Christ which passes knowledge; that you may be filled with all the fullness of God."*

You were born to be loved. If you grew up lacking the love of a mother or father, that is experienced as a trauma to your soul. If you grew up not knowing the presence of comfort or not experiencing a sense of safety or a presence of peace, that could cause an impact of trauma to your heart.

Even being consistently ignored or being raised by nannies or caregivers who were not your parents because your parents were absent, could cause deep trauma to your heart. Not having healthy attachments causes trauma. Being disrupted from your home, experiencing the death of a parent, or being put in foster care are all causes of trauma to the soul.

Chronic health issues experienced during childhood cause trauma. My (Amber's) son has a life-threatening peanut allergy. Since he was a baby, everywhere we go to eat, even when he visits friends' homes, looks very different for him. He has to be very careful about what he eats and even what kind of oils foods are cooked in. This causes a level of trauma for him, so much so that his heart will begin to race if he even smells peanut butter because of the fear attached to its presence. He knows what can happen to his body; it is life-threatening for him. Life can be so jolting, even in illness, to the point of trauma.

How many people do you know who have not experienced a deeply distressing event? How many children do you think make it past sixteen without experiencing some traumatizing event? If you even begin to research the statistics, they are staggering. Conservatively, it could be estimated that more than half of the world's population has experienced trauma.

The goal of sharing these things is to give you a broad understanding of the kinds of places where trauma may be hiding. Whether trauma stemmed from a single incident, chronic situations, or from multiple and varied events, no experience in a person's life should be devalued. Nothing in your life should ever be devalued. Your experiences are valid. Everyone handles things differently; everyone has a unique worldview. If we approach our pain and the pain of others with a heart of honor and respect, we are in the best posture to facilitate healing and freedom.

CHAPTER THREE

YOUR BRAIN

If you are fascinated by neuroscience like we are, you will love this next part. If anything with the word science in it makes you want to grab a pillow and a blanket for a quick nap, trust us, this part will even keep **you** interested. Promise yourself you will read it through and not check out. Let the Lord bring some revelation and understanding to you as you soak this information in.

Our brains play such a significant role in how trauma impacts our lives. In order to understand why you respond the way you do, you must first consider the role of the brain and the way the brain processes.

Let's start by breaking down the four main brain sections involved with processing information.

First, let's look at the **Brainstem**. The Brainstem is responsible for regulating your temperature control, breathing, keeping your heart beating, keeping your organs functioning, etc. This part of your brain is actually often referred to as the "reptilian" part of your brain by many neuroscientists because it has the same level of emotional intelligence as a reptile. Now, we would never call your brain a reptile! But we will allow the graphic imagery from our friends in the science field to paint us a picture with that almost offensive reference. The brainstem receives information from all of your senses. When you feel, taste, smell, see, or hear, that input is first registered in your brainstem.

The next part of your brain is called the **Amygdala**. The amygdala is the part of the brain that detects stress, perceives fear, and instigates a flight or fight response. This is the part of your brain that receives information from your brainstem, all the communication collected by your senses, and then begins to communicate to the rest of your brain what it *perceives* is happening. It is almost as if this part of your brain acts like a judge, or we sometimes refer to it as the gossipy little part of your brain because it tells the rest of the brain what it thinks may be happening. One way to remember the amygdala is to imagine that this part of your brain is basically playing telephone with the rest of your brain, and it may or may not be perceiving things correctly.

The **Hippocampus** is next. This is where reward, memory, bonding, learning, and emotions are housed. It connects emotion to memories. Together, the amygdala and hippocampus work to release the stress hormones of cortisol and adrenaline. If you find yourself in a constant state of feeling stressed, you can thank your hippocampus! The hippocampus is persuadable and highly influenced. A playful way to remember the hippocampus is to picture a bunch of hippos on a college campus, rushing to get to class so they can learn—a hippo in a tutu or a hippo with a letterman's jacket walking on campus. Can you see it?

The last section we are going to look at is actually the last part of your brain to develop – the **Prefrontal Cortex**. This is the part of your brain where creativity, thinking, language, reasoning, problem-solving, impulse control, perseverance, comprehension, values, beliefs, hope, and the **ability to be aware of time** are all stored. Your prefrontal cortex has a big job! And isn't it interesting that your brain doesn't finish developing until you're twenty-five years old? If impulse control is one of the last things to develop when you're already in your twenties, teenagers sure make a lot more sense, don't they?

See, that was just four short yet intriguing paragraphs, not nearly enough information for our non-science-loving friends to want to take a nap! We aren't even to the most fascinating part yet.

Take a moment and perhaps underline, highlight, or circle the part in the prefrontal cortex paragraph that says, "the ability to be aware of time." You will find great clarity if you hold on to this understanding. Our prefrontal cortex is where our brain's awareness of time resides.

Why does this matter? It's important because our brains process information in the order that the brain first developed—brainstem, amygdala, hippocampus, and prefrontal cortex. Remember that the prefrontal cortex doesn't finish developing until the mid-twenties. Understanding how our brains process from the brainstem to the cortex, the same way the brain developed, helps us understand why we think and react the way we do. When input comes into our brains (through the brainstem), our brain begins to interpret that information through stress responses (thanks to the amygdala and hippocampus) before the information has the chance to process through the reasoning center of the prefrontal cortex.

Your fear, stress, and emotional responses are triggered in your brain before your ability to think and reason are activated. Or, very importantly, these fear, stress, and emotional responses are triggered before you have the ability to know **WHEN** you are, where you are, and how old you are. Your fear triggers are activated first. Your emotional responses are activated before you even know when and where you are.

Can you relate to that? Something happens, and you begin to feel emotional, fearful, or have a stress response, and someone asks you, "Are you okay?" You may be thinking, "I don't know! I don't know yet what I'm thinking or what happened or why I feel this way." Your brain is trying to bring all the information to your prefrontal cortex to evaluate and bring understanding.

Another key component of understanding why an external cue to your senses might make you begin to feel stress that you don't understand yet is to know that memory is stored all along the timeline of our brain development and life experiences. Every part of your brain has the ability to store memory. Think about the muscle memory of being able to walk, ride a bike, or use a fork. Do you have to think intently about every step you take while you are walking to the bathroom? No. Why? It's because your body remembers. You learned how to walk when you were still an infant, and that is now stored as a muscle memory in your brain that works automatically. Every level of our brains stores memories.

Let me (Amber) give you an example. I love my Granny. She is in Heaven now. She was my sun, moon, and stars. I never got to live near her, which is perhaps why I so treasured my time with her. We got to see her maybe four or five times per year. Every time we would pull up to see her, it was always the same scene. She would be standing in her place on the patio, wearing her little duster house dress, with a tissue tucked in her watchband; she would always push her little glasses up from slipping down her nose. It really was the same scenario every time we rolled into her driveway. You could count on Granny being just as she always had been.

I would get so excited with anticipation as we got closer and closer in the car, and as we pulled up to her house, I could hardly wait for the car to stop before I would hop out and run as fast as I could up to my Granny. I would throw my arms around her and bury my face into her soft belly. Every time, I would be immediately hit with a wafting smell of Bengay, spearmint gum, and mothballs. Yep! Those were the smells of my precious Granny.

Even now, as an adult, every time I smell any of those three fragrances – Bengay, spearmint, or mothballs—I have so much memory associated with them. I will immediately see her face, remember how she looked, and feel a great deal of joy. I can also hear her voice and the way she would always say, "God love her!" I am always reminded of the feeling of being loved. Those responses are all different sections of the brain reacting to the stored memory associated with a smell.

Our brains store memories as we develop. All the things we experience through our senses can be stored in our minds as a memory. So, when you experience that same cue to your senses at a later date, your brain can activate the stored memory. What do you think of when you smell cinnamon? When you hear a song from childhood, what memories does it stir up within you? When you see that it is really cloudy outside, does it give you a hint that rain might be possible? Why? Because the last time the sky looked that way, it rained, and you remember the association between dark clouds and rainstorms. Do you touch the fire in the fireplace? I would hope not. At some point, you were taught that fire is harmful to touch. Now hopefully, you learned that in a gentle way from the loving instruction of a parent and not by getting burned, but your mind remembers either way.

Our brain is actively storing memories every moment of our lives. This includes wonderful memories like the smell of love and joy associated with Granny's hugs and spearmint gum, but it can also be true of hard and difficult things we have faced. What thoughts and emotions come to your mind when I mention the smell of a hospital? Can you see a hospital? Do you have happy memories from the birth of a child or hard memories from an accident or injury? Our memories are not just two-dimensional photographs that float through our recollection from time to time. Our memories have more dimensions to them—smells, feelings, sights, sounds, tastes – and so many potential emotional and physical reactions to those dimensions. Our mind remembers, and our body remembers, whether we have positive memories that bring warm feelings of love or hard memories that make us want to shut down and forget forever.

We are tri-part beings—spirit, mind/soul, and body. It is by gaining an understanding about the way our mind and body work together, storing our memories, and the way our brain works and works with our senses, thoughts, and emotions that we can better understand ourselves and posture ourselves to heal. If you can't connect your physical responses and emotional reactions to a "why," you might find ways to cope, but it is very challenging to heal and gain the freedom that Jesus provided. Discovering how our minds and bodies work opens up the opportunity to uncover the why behind our reactions to life. This is where true healing and freedom can come in.

Here is an insider tip we can share with you right off the bat. A significant amount of our "why's" are related to childhood. You may have noticed that we started this book with questions about your earliest memories, and we have used several references to childhood stories to bring clarity to our subject. This is very intentional. A lot of our core memories are developed in childhood and have a tremendous impact on the way we think and engage with the world around us. Essentially, our childhood education is what becomes the lens of our adulthood.

Hear us on this; this is not pop-psychology or justification for not showing up in life due to childhood hardships. This is an absolutely essential truth about the way we develop and the impact our early development has on our worldview and relating styles. Trauma experienced in early childhood and adolescence has a greater impact than trauma we might endure as adults because our brains were still forming.

Our brains form from the time we are in our mother's womb until our prefrontal cortex finishes developing around the age of twenty-five. The brain is still growing and very active in adulthood, but the primary development of our brain happens in the first two decades of our lives. Here is a fascinating fact that will help explain; babies, while they are developing, acquire tens of thousands of new neurons every single second. Every second! Tens of thousands every second! How many new neurons do you suppose you will develop today as an adult? A whopping seven hundred. You have seven hundred neurons to work with today – use them wisely! You're reading this book, so good job using some of your neurons for today to learn something new.

Babies have tens of thousands of new neurons every second; therefore, their worldview is being developed one second at a time. They are absorbing what is happening around them at a staggering rate. They learn to smile by being smiled at and absorbing that. They are learning how to move and make sounds and eventually how to walk and play and grow into childhood. It is absolutely stunning the way that God created our brains and our bodies. *"You formed my innermost being, shaping my delicate inside and my intricate outside, and wove them all together in my mother's womb"* (Psalm 139:13 TPT). We were woven together in our mother's wombs, and then at a rapid rate as babies and children, we are being written on like a blank slate. This is especially true in the first few months of life.

Did you know that you can have a baby who is well cared for in the first two months of life, who feels nurtured, attended to, secure, safe, loved, stable, regulated, and well attached; who then experiences over a decade of trauma, including, abuse and neglect, who will do better in life with resiliency and attachment than a child who may have experienced trauma or unhealthy attachment in the first two months of life followed by over a decade of stability, love, attachment, and nurture? Is that not almost unbelievable to consider? This is how critical our first months and years of life are to the development of our view of the world and of ourselves.

The experiences in the life of a child, especially in the early years, dictate the way they engage with life from that point forward. Essentially, you become the adult version of your childhood education – whether healthy or unhealthy. At this point in our lives, much has already been written on our minds, many good things and perhaps some not-so-great things. What does it stir in you to think about what might have been written on your heart at the tender infant and childhood stages of your life? Do you think perhaps there may still be places where you need those writings upon your heart to be rewritten by the tender, loving hand of the Lord? Or can you connect with some really positive things that may have been written upon your heart?

I (Amber) can give you a funny example. To preface, I may or may not use the word "poop," so if that is offensive to you at all, I'm very sorry; please feel free to skip to the end of this chapter. It just really drives home this point.

When my firstborn son, Spencer, was born, I did not receive an owner's manual. You just have to learn, and it is on-the-job training. Before Spencer was born, my husband and I had a whole conversation about how we were going to handle diaper changes. Generally, this job tends to fall on the mom. No matter who is holding the baby, the minute there is a diaper change needed, the baby is brought to the mom. I protested this idea! My rebuttal was, "No! If it happens in your arms, you're responsible for diaper duty. Don't bring it to me." So that became our agreement.

Well, Spencer was brand new, a brand-new baby boy. The nurses had warned me about something that was going to happen in his diaper about an hour after he was born; they told me about how the first bowel movements of an infant are meconium, and it is a very "unique" experience. They just so happened to share this information with me while my husband, Stephen, was not in the room. I kept that information to myself and didn't tell him. Soon after, he was holding our baby in the hospital room. All of a sudden, there was a loud sound, that resembled a small explosion, in our son's diaper. It startled my husband so intensely that he looked wide-eyed at me and shockingly questioned,

"What was that?!" and he started to bring the baby to me.

I immediately responded, "No sir, that was not our deal! You have to change him."

As Stephen opened the diaper, his face was afraid and contorted and apprehensive, and he was exclaiming, "Ugh! What is that? This is so gross! It looks like tar!"

At that very moment, I got pricked in my heart, and I said, "Stop that!"

"What? Stop what?" he replied.

"That!" I said, "We can't do that! We can't make those faces; we can't make those facial expressions to the baby when we are changing him. It is going to make him think something bad has happened or something is wrong. It could cause constipation or any myriad of other problems. You have to change your facial expressions!"

I was suddenly thinking of all these issues it could cause to our baby down the road if he thought going to the bathroom was somehow wrong or disgusting. My baby could get plugged up thinking something was wrong. But it was the Holy Spirit. Holy Spirit was helping me even though I didn't fully understand, but my baby's worldview was beginning to develop right at that moment. The message being offered was that going poo was something that wasn't good. Eventually, the baby would connect displeasure with that facial expression. So, I would correct my mom or anyone who would be helping with the baby. I would tell them, "If he does a number two, please just smile, if you don't mind, and don't make any negative sounds. That would be great." They thought it was strange, but I just reassured them I had my reasons.

Changing my baby's diaper was a bonding moment, no matter whether I was choking back a gag or not. I loved my children and wanted them to feel cherished at every moment. Now, as teenagers, both of my boys feel very secure in their bodies. There is no shame associated with any of their bodily functions. There is no shyness, nothing. Normal bodily function is common conversation around our home.

Worldview is incredibly significant. As human beings, we are being written on by the world around us from the very second we are born. What messages were written upon your mind? What do you think about the complex collection of memories that have been etched upon your brain to make you into the person you are today? Can you see the connection between the way you were educated about the world as a child and the adult perspective you have today?

We celebrate with you the beautiful, Godly things that were written upon your life. As we move forward into the next chapters, we are also going to walk you through some very practical steps you can take to partner with God's healing, if there were things written upon your life that you know were not His plan for you.

CHAPTER FOUR

STRESS

How busy was your day today? Or, if you are reading this in the morning, how busy is your day going to be today? I (Rachel) was talking to my mother on the phone earlier today, trying to see if we could squeeze in a quick coffee break to see each other as we navigated through our full schedules. We hopped on the phone in between appointments as we were both in our separate cars. We took turns giving each other a run-down of our calendar to see if we could find a space where we both had a gap at the same time. It turned out that we found a thirty-minute window to squeeze in this afternoon. Out of seven days in a week, a hundred and sixty-eight hours, ten thousand and eighty minutes…we found thirty. That was almost a miracle. Does life ever feel that complicated to you?

It is incredible how full our schedules can be, as a culture, just trying to keep up with all the things that make us responsible adults: making time with the Lord an absolute priority, paying attention to our marriages, caring for our children, our families, our homes, and our community, and trying to be good humans and examples of God's love to the world around us. And at the end of the day, we are lying in bed at night hoping we did a good job today, hoping we were kind enough and loving enough to the people around us, thanking God for all He did, and asking Him to meet us with His grace again tomorrow.

It is a balance, though, because there is a difference between full, busy, and downright stressful. Stress is a whole other ballgame. Stress happens when life's circumstances begin to get outside of what is reasonable, and pressure begins to build. When stress is sustained for long periods of time without coming back into balance, it begins to affect our health. Stress can affect our hormones, our blood pressure, and our sleep, and it can cause weight gain because of increased cortisol levels, as well as weaken our immune systems. Ongoing, sustained stress is not ideal for our well-being. Stress is also a primary component of trauma. Trauma essentially begins as a stressor.

Before we discuss the way trauma and stress are related, it is important to clarify that not all stress is bad. Stress in the form of challenges is what promotes our growth as humans. In order to grow and develop resiliency for life, we need to be challenged by stressors. Babies need to be challenged to learn to roll over, sit up, walk, feed themselves, and eventually be potty trained. These can feel like stressful events to little ones, but without a baby facing these stressful developmental challenges, you would be changing your otherwise capable teenager's diaper. No one wants to think about how awful that would be.

Kids also need to be challenged in school in order to grow and develop their minds and bodies. **Development happens when stressors are faced and overcome.** Athletes are also an example of people who engage with positive stressors. Think about how they have to challenge their bodies and hone their skills to grow and become successful at their sport. As humans, we need to be challenged in order to grow – this is healthy stress. When it can be conquered, the goal achieved, and resiliency cultivated, stress has a healthy and helpful form. If you, as an adult, still felt just as challenged as you did when you were first learning to walk, there would be a problem. If you never overcame the challenge of learning to add and subtract, read, or run, the stressors of life would seem insurmountable. We grow and develop by facing stressors and successfully mastering them. What starts as a stressor becomes a skill that marks growth in us. This process of learning should be continual for our entire lifetime.

However, stress has a form that can actually feel insurmountable. When we are put into repetitive stressful situations that seem uncontrollable or inescapable, trauma can begin to form. When stress becomes extreme, it becomes distressing. Distressing situations that we are exposed to over and over again can cause trauma. Even singular, deeply distressing events cause trauma. Trauma begins as a stressor that, at some point, became overwhelming. While repetitive life stress can cause issues with our health, when we encounter repetitive, overwhelming stressors, it can begin to cause trauma to our brains and to our souls.

"The spirit of a man will sustain him in sickness; but who can bear a broken spirit?" (Proverbs 18:14).

God created us with the ability to face trials that allow us to grow and develop. When the things we face stem from sin or are outside the created order of God, it becomes wounding to our vessels. We are not designed to live in the pool of other people's sins. Being ongoingly subjected to the sin of others, especially when it is inescapable, can cause trauma.

Child abuse causes trauma – every form of child abuse.
Being neglected causes trauma.
Witnessing someone being held at gunpoint causes trauma.
School shootings cause trauma.
Parents getting divorced causes trauma.
Being bullied causes trauma.
Facing a severe illness causes trauma.

The list could go on, but can you see the connection between trauma-inducing events and the heart of God for His children? None of these things are born from the heart of God. We are not meant to endure them. They are born from the hellish schemes of the Enemy; they aren't meant to be part of our lives, and there is a consequence to that. Trauma is often the result—the consequence—that we are marked with.

So how do we know when we have gone from a stressor that we can overcome to an insurmountable distressing place that may have resulted in trauma? Well, there are several indicators that we may be carrying trauma. Some of them are very practical and evident even in our physical responses to situations.

Our bodies actually have two primary responses to excessive stress. The first response to stress is what is known as the **Arousal State,** or more commonly known as **Fight or Flight**. When our body is in a state of Fight or Flight, most of the blood in our bodies rushes to our extremities. Our hearts begin to race, and adrenaline is released in order to assist us in an escape or a fight.

Have you heard of fight or flight? It is pretty common, and most people are familiar with this term. However, did you also know that we actually go through four stages instead of just two? The first thing we do in this arousal state is actually to **flock**. We flock by looking around to make eye contact with our safe people; we flock to them. Think about the first thing you would do if you heard a noise in the middle of the night. You would likely wake up your spouse and say, "Babe did you hear that? Listen!" Or, let's say there was a tornado headed towards your house; you would immediately think about gathering all your family members. When a toddler falls down, they turn and look to their mom or dad to see whether they are okay or not, and the toddler often responds based on the parent's response. We flock first.

The second thing we do in an arousal state is **freeze**. What would you and your spouse do right after you locked eyes following an unusual noise in the middle of the night? You would probably freeze and shallow breathe so you could be quiet enough to hear that noise again. Freeze is the pause while your mind is catching up and trying to get all the information to your prefrontal cortex, so you can determine what your next move should be.

Our next response is to try to **flee**. If there was a tornado coming towards your house, you flock to your loved ones, take a moment to determine what to do, and immediately try to flee to a safe place. Our adrenaline instinct is to get away from danger and to remove our loved ones from danger. This is true whether it is real or perceived danger. Sometimes when we have been through trauma, the amygdala, that gossipy little part of our brain, tells us there is danger when there really isn't. Even when you are surrounded by people who love and care about you very much, the amygdala can tell you there is danger, and keep you in a constant state of needing to flee because you don't feel safe. In fact, this feeling is coming from old information, stemming from trauma. We will talk more about this in the coming chapters.

The final stage of the arousal state is to **fight**. If you don't believe you will be able to get away from the danger you're facing, your body prepares to fight. It releases adrenaline to help you protect yourself and fight off danger. Do you know anybody who seems to always be in a fight or flight state? Fight or Flight can actually become such a habit in our brains because of trauma and overwhelming stressors that we can stay in an activated arousal state. It feels like drinking twenty shots of espresso all the time. There is no sense of peace. Adrenaline and cortisol are pumping through your body constantly. This can play out in the way we relate to others as well. The more we are in a state of stress that keeps us in an arousal state, the more likely the people around us are to encounter the flight or fight version of us, and it can cause relational damage.

The second primary response to excessive stress is **Dissociation**. When you have become convinced you cannot flee and you won't survive the "fight," the next response our bodies offer us is dissociation. In this state, you pull back into yourself. Your body actually pulls all the blood from your extremities, pulls it towards your core to protect your organs, and releases its own pain-reducing opiates as it prepares to endure injury. Your heart rate decreases to preserve your blood. It looks like shutting down, pulling into your mind, and "checking out" or becoming numb to your environment.

Much like our bodies have a healthy use for stress as we learn and grow, we also have a healthy use for stress responses. Our natural stress responses are meant to be a gift to us as we navigate through life circumstances and build our resiliency. Fight or flight helps us to escape dangerous situations— imagine the response needed to pull your child away from the street if a car was coming in their direction. The adrenaline release is meant to help us in situations that are dangerous.

This is also true for dissociation. We go through a subtle form of dissociation, more specifically a partial dissociation, when we daydream or read a book and escape into a different place. For example, when athletes "dig deep" as they feel physical discomfort, they are partially dissociating to press past their wall and reach a goal. Partial dissociation is also helpful when you are at the dentist and want your mind to be able to think about something besides the drill in your tooth. Think about a mother giving birth; she is focused on the treasure at the end of her pain in order to press through the excruciating agony her body is enduring.

What happens, though, when stressors escalate in frequency and intensity? When someone experiences repeated exposure to distressing events, the stress responses are being employed so often that the responses become more extreme and more easily triggered. This is especially true during development. Imagine you are in a public place, and you hear someone suddenly begin shouting. You might flock, maybe even freeze, until you realize that they were trying to get someone's attention across the room, and there is no danger present. You may go back to what you were doing and not be bothered anymore by it. However, now imagine that you grew up in a very verbally abusive household where yelling happened all the time – that one instance of yelling, even though it wasn't directed at you, might cause a tremendous deal of stress.

Our ability to handle stress is dependent upon how sensitive we are to the stressor itself. Picture your soul as a bucket, whatever style bucket, vase, or container you want to imagine. If your bucket is empty and someone splashes a little water on you, you can absorb it, pour it out at the Lord's feet, and move on with your day. However, if your bucket is full from all the things that have already been poured on you that were more than you were designed to carry, how much capacity do you think you would have to carry more stressors from life happening around you? One, even incidental, thing being poured on you might feel overwhelming and cause a mess of overflow everywhere around you.

Sometimes that full bucket can become so overwhelming, and dissociation can be employed so often, that it becomes a way of life. It can become habitual, where the person isn't even aware that it is happening. It can present in a person in such a way that they believe their emotions to simply be numb. They can feel distant from identifiers about their life, almost as if when their past is mentioned, it feels like it is referring to someone else. We have ministered to so many people who have endured so much trauma, especially in their childhood, that they have fractured parts of their souls and need healing. This happens when dissociation was employed so strongly that whole parts of their memory shut down, completely removing their awareness of that memory. We will talk more about soul fractures in a later section of this book, but we wanted you to see the connection between overwhelming life events and eventual soul fractures.

An indicator that you might be carrying trauma is sensitivity to stressors. If you reach your capacity to cope much quicker than what might be considered normal, there is likely a reason for it. Could you be carrying trauma in your mind, body, and soul that you don't even realize has been there since your youth?

This response is often referred to as a trigger. When a person becomes dysregulated, or the body is not controlled the way it normally would be, because an evocative cue (an external signal that prompts a physical or emotional response in connection to a specific memory) sets off their stress response, that is what is referred to as a trigger. We are going to discuss triggers further in the next chapter, but it is important to understand their connection with stressors.

Understanding the way that stress impacts and can cause trauma is essential for healing from trauma. The more we understand, the easier it becomes to partner with the Lord as He leads us toward healing.

CHAPTER FIVE

TRIGGERS

Picture an absolutely gorgeous day outside. The sunshine is hugging your skin. There is a gentle breeze dancing gracefully through the atmosphere. You're walking down the sidewalk with your closest friends, laughing and chatting as you head to your favorite lunch spot. There is no pressure in this day, no stress, just joy. Your heart feels such gratitude and delight at the blessings of life all around you. Can you see it? Can you feel it? Imagine.

In your joy on such a pleasant day, you decide to head out for a bite to eat with your friends. As you turn to go into the restaurant, your chest begins to tighten. What? Suddenly you're finding it difficult to breathe. Your palms begin to sweat. Why? A few seconds later, you realize your heart is racing. There's so much pressure in your chest that you wonder if you might be having a heart attack. Your heart feels like it could explode. You begin to get really dizzy, and the room feels like it is spinning. All of these sensations seem to be hitting your body at one time. You begin to panic! "What is wrong with me?" Your mind is racing. "What is happening? Breathe. I just need to breathe. Why can't I breathe? I can't seem to get any air! My chest hurts so bad. What is going on?" This is what a trigger can feel like.

It takes twenty minutes for your heart rate to calm down and for you to feel like you can breathe again. Only now, you feel embarrassed because your friends are all looking at you with concern when half an hour ago you were having the best day. What just happened? You aren't even sure yourself.

Perhaps you start to feel better for a while, and then it all begins to escalate again. Like waves that come and crash against a shore, you spend a whole day experiencing episodes of extreme negative sensations in your body, just hoping they will stop completely at some point.

This is an example of what a triggered state can feel like, going from a perfectly lovely day to suddenly feeling like your body is in a crisis, even when you don't understand why. Can you imagine it? Have you ever experienced it for yourself?

Other forms of a triggered state could present in more subtle ways. For instance, you may hear a familiar song playing over the speakers while you are at the grocery store, and suddenly, you have the urge to just leave your basket full of groceries and get out of the store.

You might hear fireworks going off and impulsively hit the ground and cover your head because you grew up in an area full of violence or were in the military and experienced combat.

A trigger is what happens when a person becomes dysregulated. Being dysregulated means a person's body responses are not as easily controlled as they normally would be. This usually happens when an evocative cue sets off a person's stress response.

Here is what is happening during a trigger. The place within the brain that experienced trauma can be activated into a visceral reaction when it is brushed up against by an evocative cue, something familiar to the traumatic event. This could be a smell, a sound, a familiar feeling, a thought, an image, or basically anything that can be perceived by your senses and translated to the brain as reminiscent of the trauma that was experienced.

The smell of old spice might be the smell associated with a person who was an abuser, and every time that fragrance hits your nose, your brain experiences those vivid memories all over again. Remember the smell of mothballs, spearmint gum, and Bengay from my (Amber's) Granny? My memories associated with those smells evoke a very real emotion of joy. But for someone who experienced trauma, familiar smells may bring a very real feeling of terror or torment because of the memory associated with that smell.

If I (Rachel) closed my eyes and smelled a balsam and cedar candle, my mind would immediately see Christmas trees. I would almost be able to hear laughter and Christmas music. My mind would play images of Christmases past, eliciting a sigh of gratitude and joy.

What would come to your mind if I asked what memories you have associated with:
- Ice cream
- Your birthday
- Sundays
- Summer
- Dogs
- Snow
- Swimming
- Family

If you actually stopped and allowed your mind to engage with these words, I am guessing you just had a whole slew of images dance across the screen of your mind. Did the thought of ice cream on a warm summer day almost make your mouth water? Do you love swimming or have a fear of the water? Do you love dogs, or maybe you had a bad experience with one? The thoughts that came to your mind are memories of your own experiences or maybe even images you have seen associated with those words.

Memories are so powerful. A whole slew of emotions, images, and memories can become attached to a simple word. Imagine how much more powerful those memories are when they are connected to the actual experience of our senses. Any cue to our senses can trigger our entire nervous system.

I (Rachel) have a slightly terrible example of this. The summer that I was twelve, I spent a lot of time with one of my aunts. It was a Saturday evening, and we had spent the day running errands and shopping. She was grilling hamburgers for us that night, and we were going to watch a movie.

35

My aunt, her eight-year-old son, and I ate dinner, cleaned it up, finished doing our chores, and settled down to watch a movie. Before the movie was even over, all three of us were fighting over the bathrooms in the house, and sometimes settling for the trash can! I think I threw up for nearly six hours straight. I don't know if I ever fully left the bathroom that night. I've never been that violently ill in my life, nor would I want to be! I will spare you the gruesome details, but I will tell you that it took me over thirteen years before I would ever eat a hamburger again. Thirteen years! I couldn't even handle seeing a commercial on television with a hamburger on it (And yes, we still had commercials when I was younger, ha!) One sight or smell of a hamburger, and I would contemplate running for the bathroom because my gag reflex was so triggered. All this to say, a visceral reaction to a triggered memory is a very real thing.

I (Amber) think it is quite coincidental that Rachel took thirteen years to eat a hamburger because it reminds me of what happened to me on my thirteenth birthday. I loved watermelon... all things watermelon. Watermelon ChapStick, lotion, candy, and shampoo were my favorites. I even had watermelon scratch and sniff stickers. Watermelon was my thing. So for my thirteenth birthday, my parents threw me a watermelon-themed birthday party. All of my friends brought a watermelon. Why not? It was my favorite thing. We had a seed-spitting contest and a watermelon-eating contest. So much watermelon was consumed at my party.

Then, my father, being the fun, engaging dad that he was, decided to have all the kids climb up on one of those old metal merry-go-rounds. We all piled on. It was the type of merry-go-round that you had to hold onto with a vice grip, or you would definitely go flying off. My dad got that thing going so fast! We were having the best time, laughing and squealing with delight. Until suddenly, we weren't. All of a sudden, we needed the thing to stop. We were all starting to yell at him to please let us off! I got so sick...**So sick!** I threw up to such an extreme, I still haven't eaten watermelon again to this day. And let me just tell you, it has been much longer than 13 years. I even walk quickly past the watermelon section at the supermarket, so many years later.

What is happening to our brain when a memory is triggered? When our brain creates a memory of an event, our nervous system's response mechanism creates a physical memory right in tandem with the event memory. If I have a memory of having food poisoning, or watermelon overload, my body's nervous system has a memory as well. Now, every time the memory of that event is activated, the nervous system's responses to that memory are also activated.

This is how trauma is stored in the brain.

A physical response, a smell, a taste, a sound, or any nervous system response can be stored as an evocative cue associated with a memory of an event. When that evocative cue is triggered at a later time, that input goes into our senses and triggers the brain stem. Our brain stem begins to react to the input from the frame of reference of what it remembers—not what is happening right now. The brain stem functions without the added information from the prefrontal cortex. (Remember that information about time, reason, beliefs, and thoughts are stored at the front of the brain in the prefrontal cortex.) After the information hits the brainstem, it travels up through the part of your brain that perceives fear, the amygdala. Then it goes to the part of your brain that controls emotions, the hippocampus. And finally, it travels to the part of your mind that regulates thoughts, time, and beliefs, the prefrontal cortex.

Understand that your nervous system begins to respond to the evocative cue that just triggered your memory from the state where the memory was first created, before your prefrontal cortex gets a chance to tell you when and where you are. Before you get a chance to tell yourself that you are okay and not in the place of that memory any longer, your nervous system reacts.

This is **ESSENTIAL** to grasp because a state of being triggered is not a rational state. When you are experiencing a trigger, you are not reasonable. You are likely in the process of trying to come out of the memory your brain just temporarily thrust you into. You cannot successfully reason with someone in a triggered state. That also means you should be gracious to not expect yourself to be able to be completely rational until you have come out of the trauma-triggered state.

What does a trauma-triggered state look like?

When a trauma memory stored within your brain has been triggered, it can present itself in a variety of ways, such as shortness of breath, dizziness, sweating, muscle tension, shaking, ringing in the ears, a sense of doom or panic, chest tightness, chest pain, the sensation of having a heart attack, increased heart rate, intense fear, or the lack of feeling safe. It can make you feel like you are dying, or it can be more subtle, like having a sense of urgency to simply get up and leave the room.

For instance, trauma triggers for an abused child may present as an intense fear of seeing someone who looks similar to their abuser or recoiling from touch of any kind. These triggers may be more obvious, while subtle triggers often go unrecognized or dismissed because they don't escalate to something besides minor discomfort. Sometimes triggers can even come from the build-up of stress in the day-to-day responsibilities of life.

The point is that triggers can be an indicator of the presence of unresolved trauma, however the triggers manifest, whether subtle or extreme. If the body's nervous system is responding to an evocative cue, and if the stress responses are being deployed, there may be an outward demonstration of an internal place of trauma that needs to be resolved.

We may not have mentioned your exact trauma response or triggered state. We may not have specifically covered the situation in your life that caused you to experience trauma, but please don't let that discount your situation. What you have experienced is valid! What you may be experiencing now, through triggered moments, matters to the heart of God! We implore you to lean into the Holy Spirit and allow Him to highlight any area in your life where you may need healing from trauma. His witness is what you need, and He is the Healer! He is the Great Physician, and He longs to heal you more than you can possibly imagine.

CHAPTER SIX

DEMONS

We have a little exercise to help us dive into this absolutely vital section of this book. It is going to require that you use your imagination. Okay, let's practice. Picture in your mind a beautiful sunset. Really paint the details in there. Let's imagine that a storm just passed, and the sky is full of clouds, the sunlight reflecting on the clouds in magnificent shades of orange, yellow, pink, purple, and blue. Maybe you're on a hilltop, and you can see the wide expanse of landscape beneath you. You're watching as the colors in the sky are also dusting the trees and fields with similar hues. Can you see it? Are you envisioning a beautifully painted masterpiece? Good job!

Now that you are warmed up, this is the visual we want you to paint in your mind. Are you ready? Great. We want you to picture a giant zit. Yes, on purpose. A giant zit. Really get a good visual. We are talking about the kind of zit with a red ring around the outside and the whitehead about to burst. (Also, why do they call it a whitehead when we all know it is a disgusting color of yellow threatening to burst out in pus?) The skin is tight and agitated, causing discomfort all around its location. Can you see it? You might not know whether to pop the thing or plaster it with caution tape. Is it making you nauseated to think about it yet? Do you have a good visual for reference? Great!

What in the world does a giant zit have to do with trauma? Well, a zit is a very effective visual to aid in understanding the relationship between trauma and deliverance. The activity of the Enemy is very much like the disgusting collection of bacteria and dead skin cells that make up the pus in a zit. The thin layer of skin over the infected pore is the trauma that is keeping the collection of the Enemy's pus attached to the person. Being healed from trauma often requires the expulsion of the demonic schemes of the Devil connected with the traumatic events.

One of the most effective schemes of the Enemy is his efforts to demonize mankind. Satan and his horde of evil spirits seek to oppress, infest, and possess the minds and bodies of humans. It is effective because it goes widely unrecognized or dismissed as character issues or personality flaws. All the while, we are actually wrestling against an invisible enemy, and we often aren't even aware of the battle we are in. *"For we do not wrestle against flesh and blood, but against principalities, against powers, against the rulers of the darkness of this age, against spiritual hosts of wickedness in the heavenly places"* (Ephesians 6:12). We need to become aware because healing and freedom are attached to our willingness to become aware and allow the Lord to move on our behalf.

Demons are evil spirits looking for a body to enter into so that they might fulfill their evil nature. For instance, A demon of lust is looking for a body to enter so that it might express its lustful nature. A spirit of fear is looking to enter a body and create fear that paralyzes the person, that causes timidity and threatens the sanity of a person's thoughts. The Word of God says, *"For God has not given us a spirit of fear, but of power of love and of a sound mind"* (2 Timothy 1:7). A spirit of fear is not from God, but a spirit of fear is real and seeks to attach itself to our mind and thoughts.

Demons are crafty. They are wicked and manipulative. Think of all the beautiful qualities of our beloved Jesus, and then imagine the extreme opposite. In that pit of depravity, you will discover the attributes of demons. Where Jesus is love, peace, and patience, the Enemy is hatred, chaos, and ruthlessness. Demons are an expression of that wickedness. There are attributes to their nature that are often underestimated. They have a will of their own. They have emotions. They have intellect; it was a demon who spoke out of a man claiming Jesus was the Holy One of God in Mark 1:24. They have self-awareness; you can ask them their name, and they know who they are. In Mark 5:9, Legion told Jesus his name and declared the fact that there were many with him in the body of the man they were possessing. Out of that passage, you can also glean the fact that they have the ability to speak through a person's mouth. They are aggressive and try to pick fights with angels (Daniel 10:13). And you should know that if you try to stand against a demon and you are not doing so under the direction of God, it might try to rip your clothes off and beat you silly (Acts 19:16). Instead, come against the demonic with the mind of Christ, a will surrendered to God, a heart that loves Jesus, and a spirit baptized with the Holy Ghost because you don't want to get your clothes snatched off, and you want to make sure the devil is the only one leaving with a black eye and bruised behind.

Even believers in Jesus Christ can have demons. That might be shocking for some people to realize. Somehow, we ended up with an incomplete theology that claims that a believer cannot have demons and that, as children of God, we are immune. Maybe you haven't learned about the activity of demons at all. The reality of the situation is that we are the center of the Enemy's target! Churches across the world can be hiding places for the oppressive tactics of demons without even realizing it, resulting in Christians living under the weight of demonic oppression in areas that are completely unnecessary. The reality is that demons are paralyzed by those who know who they are in Christ. As Christians, we are meant to be battle ready and victorious, you have to know who you are (Ephesians 6).

How is it possible that a believer can have a demon? Can we offer some questions to ponder in an effort to help reconcile that question? It may be new for you to even explore, and that is okay, but we encourage you to lean in and ask the Holy Spirit to testify of His truth regarding this issue.

Do you believe a demon can be in a person before salvation? Where do the demons go when the person gets saved? Do most believers you know have a testimony of demons lifting from their bodies and minds at the moment of salvation? If not, is it possible that the moment of salvation involves the person's spirit, and the mind/soul/heart, and body might still need deliverance? You can own property and still need to evict squatters. In the same way, you can give God your life and still be in need of His power to clean certain rooms where the enemy has taken up residence.

Let's carry this further for more understanding of how the enemy gains access. Do you believe the enemy can give you thoughts from him? Where are your thoughts located? Aren't they located in your mind, and isn't your mind located in your body? Yes! Through question and answer, you can see proof that your mind is within your body, and your mind is what the enemy seeks to manipulate as it is the control room of your whole vessel.

When someone is sick, and fellow believers gather around the person to pray, isn't it very common to pray against the "spirit of infirmity"? Where is that spirit manifesting? Usually, sickness is evident in the person's body. So many illnesses can be caused by demons.

One of the most compelling scriptures in the New Testament, showing that a believer can have a demon, is Acts 5:3 (NIV), *"Peter said, 'Ananias, how is it that Satan has so filled your heart that you have lied to the Holy Spirit?'"* We have every reason to believe Ananias was a spirit-filled believer, and Peter is asking how Satan filled his heart.

I Corinthians 6:19 "Or do you not know that your body is the temple of the Holy Spirit who is in you, whom you have from God, and you are not your own." Here, Paul refers to us as the temple of the Holy Spirit. The temple was designed with three parts – the outer court, the inner court, and the Holy of Holies.

We are spirit, soul, and body. The outer court is our bodies. The inner court is comprised of our soul, mind, and heart; and the Holy of Holies is our spirit. The Holy Spirit dwells in our spirit, and no evil spirit can dwell where the Holy Spirit is residing. It is our body and soul that the Enemy tries to penetrate. Sin cannot enter into the Holy of Holies, but it can enter into the outer court. Demonization happens in layers. The Enemy comes from the outside in, from the outer courts, seeking to take territory all the way into the inner courts. In contrast, Jesus comes into our "Holy of Holies" in our spirit and sanctifies us from the inside out. The Holy Spirit wants to sanctify us wholly. I Thessalonians 5:23 says, *"Now may the God of peace Himself sanctify you completely; and may your whole spirit, soul, and body be preserved blameless at the coming of our Lord Jesus Christ."*

The Enemy is on the hunt to oppress us at any level. It starts on the outer layer as thoughts that set themselves against the Word of God. If a person's will comes into agreement with that thought, it becomes a belief or a stronghold and takes up more territory in the person's mind than a fleeting thought that could have been dismissed like an annoying fly. Now it has become ingrained into the person's mind. The purpose of the Enemy is to take up more and more territory from thoughts and beliefs to behavior, actions, and habits until he is so interwoven he is on the level of "Legion" and has taken control of a person's mind and life. This is why the Bible tells us to take our thoughts captive.

"For though we walk in the flesh, we do not war according to the flesh. For the weapons of our warfare are not carnal but mighty in God for pulling down strongholds, casting down arguments and every high thing that exalts itself against the knowledge of God, bringing every thought into captivity to the obedience of Christ" (2 Corinthians 10:3-5).

It is also important to realize that the Enemy sets himself up to oppress people from as young of an age as possible. He is looking for the earliest possible moments in our lives to bring oppression and demonize us so that we don't have a conscious memory of life without him. For instance, if we think that our propensity towards fear is part of our personality, the demons who are seeking to oppress us remain hidden. The Enemy will start his attacks as far back in the bloodline of our generations as he possibly can. The Enemy seeks to bring oppression from our youth and then add layer upon layer of similar themes throughout our lives to trap us in his webs of deceit, heaviness, and destruction. All the while, he accuses us of being flawed, weak, lacking in faith, or any other myriad of accusations that point our struggle's root to anything but his tactics.

If possible, childhood is where the Enemy's involvement with trauma initially comes into play. This is also why we talk so much about the trauma that happens in the early years of life and the impact it has on us as we develop into adults. Not only does trauma's impact write upon our worldview and shape our development, but the Enemy's agenda to demonize us is interwoven into those places of trauma in our brain and in our development as well. Remember the zit and its layers? That is how demonic activity becomes a part of our lives. In places of our brain, our soul, and in our bodies where trauma has taken root, the Enemy seeks to take up residence. The Enemy is a bully, and he does not play fair.

How does this happen? Well, in the moment of a traumatic event, the Enemy may be looking to attach through connection with another person. For instance, a demon of lust on a perpetrator may seek to attach to the victim of a violation. It's absolutely unjust but true nonetheless. A spirit of fear, bitterness, hatred, anger, murder, or suicide may be offering thoughts to a person in response to a trauma they experienced. It only takes the person's agreement with those thoughts to begin to open the door for demons to attach themselves. Our will is expressed through our agreement, and the Lord has humbled Himself to not violate our will. That means that when we come into agreement with the Enemy, we open the door to the Enemy's tactics and give him permission to function in our lives. Our agreement is like a wide-open door for the Enemy to come into our lives and cause destruction and turmoil. He loves it too. The Enemy is attracted to violence. He is a disgusting punk. He is like a shark, and violence is like chum to him.

The Enemy can attach to the physical body where trauma was experienced. Trauma can become trapped in the body, and demons can seek to hide there. It is heart-wrenching to watch God's precious children sometimes shake and often weep and wail while trauma is being released from their physical bodies.

Demons also may be seeking to attach through the beliefs or thoughts that infiltrate at that moment of trauma. We are talking about layers of demonic activity, a pre-planned, multi-pronged attack, instigated so that the person never gains freedom from the pain of memories associated with the trauma they experienced. A person might think he is just experiencing anxiety when in actuality, there are demons attached to trauma, causing torment. The anxiety is the guard to protect the trauma and keep it in place so that the person never heals. Imagine an onion sliced open. The trauma is at the center, and the Enemy wants to bring in layers and layers of demonic activity so you never get free of the trauma. Demons may come in through the experience itself, and more demons come through the belief system that nothing will change and there is no escape. The internal dialogue sounds like, "I'm never going to be any different. I'll never be free. There is no hope for me. Nothing I do seems to help."

Strongholds are being established through thoughts, and more demons seek to attach to the trauma point so that freedom is harder to attain.

Fear, for instance, is typically the first response to a traumatic event. It seems reasonable to experience fear in the moment of trauma. It's right to be cautious. The event was not ok; it was startling. The Enemy wants to abominate the very real feeling of being startled by a traumatic event and turn it into an agreement giving permission to a spirit of fear. The spirit of fear is a gatekeeper. It comes in and holds open a gate that allows more demons to attach by our agreement with whatever it is telling us to be afraid of. It wants to take control over our nervous system and lock the experience into our physical being, to trap it there and set up house.

The desire of the Enemy is to be so deeply embedded through trauma in a person's life that he schemes to take complete possession of their identity. The goal is to get the person to agree with his version of them. You can tell when a person has reached this point by statements such as, "Well, I have always just been a fearful person. It is just who I am. I've always been overly cautious. I've always been timid. I've always had anxiety." The Enemy will talk to you in first person so you think it is your own thoughts, your own ideas. In reality, it is him seeking to keep you bound by talking to you in a narrative that sounds like yourself.

The Enemy comes in during moments of trauma and offers his counsel of despair. He is attempting to present to you an interpretation of the events, of your value, and of what your worldview should be. What he is looking for is your agreement. If he can get your agreement, if he succeeds and positions himself in a place of counselor, the door is wide open for his tactics and strategies of death and destruction to influence your life. In the next chapter, we will zero in on some of the most stealthy and deadly tactics he uses against people who have suffered trauma.

CHAPTER SEVEN

SILENT KILLERS

While it is not hard to see the presence of the devil at work when murder, anger, or rage are manifesting, often times, the most common demons attached to trauma go unrecognized. They are silent predators. Let us preface by saying these are not the only demonic strategies present in trauma, but they are some of the most prevalent adversaries.

Shame and rejection are two heavy hitters when it comes to the Enemy's strategies associated with trauma. Shame comes in and points at the trauma we have experienced or the pain in our lives and tells us we deserve what has happened to us. The script of shame is written to convince you that you are damaged goods. It paints the picture of your life telling you that you are broken, flawed, wrong, and deserving of the terrible things you have endured. When our hearts are so devastated by what has happened to us that we cannot seem to reconcile the happenings of our life with any kind of reasoning that feels peaceful, shame points the finger at us and tells us we are the problem, and as such, our situations are deserved.

Shame wants to isolate you. It wants to whisper deceit into your mind and tell you that you better keep yourself hidden so no one discovers how terrible you actually are. Shame is a liar. Shame is an accuser. It not only accuses you of being hopelessly damaged, wrong, and broken, but it also accuses the Blood of Christ of not being strong enough to heal you. Shame can try to sneak into your life by posturing itself as humility, but true humility is not thinking lowly of yourself as shame would suppose. True humility is thinking properly of your value. You are incredibly valuable because of Jesus's sacrifice to rescue you. Shame wants to accuse Jesus's rescue of not being enough; it whispers to you that not even the love and sacrificial Blood of Christ can fix what is wrong with you. What an absolute lie. Don't believe it!

"In you, Lord my God, I put my trust. I trust in you; do not let me be put to shame, nor let my enemies triumph over me. No one who hopes in you will ever be put to shame, but shame will come on those who are treacherous without cause" (Psalms 25:1-3 NIV).

Shame is so powerful in its influence because it holds hands with its buddy, rejection. The reason shame can be such a stronghold is because it tells you that if people knew how flawed you really were, they would reject you. Rejection is incredibly painful. We will all naturally brush up against rejection throughout our lives. Not getting a job you applied for or having a dating relationship dissolve may cause feelings of rejection. All kinds of things we face in life give us opportunities to bounce back from moments of rejection, but these moments are not the same as being under the oppression of a spirit of rejection.

A spirit of rejection, when we have come into agreement with it, is an absolutely beastly tormenter. It makes a person constantly feel like they have to walk on eggshells around everyone. This spirit makes every little nuance of another person's behavior seem like a personal attack against you. Rejection is a terrible interpreter of situations in general. It accuses both you and the people you are in relationship with at the same time. It constantly suspects the behavior and words of other people as being directed at you in a disdainful way. It misinterprets every encounter through a lens of over-sensitivity that ends with you feeling alone, abandoned, and rejected as unworthy. Can you see how rejection is such a companion of shame?

Rejection bullies you with the fear of being discarded. It lies to you and pokes your emotions, trying to cause pain with its lying scripts of others' assessments of you, resulting in abandonment. Its goal is to isolate and torment you. It isolates you by telling you to pull away from others so that they don't abandon you. Meanwhile, when you do pull away from others, it also seeks to make those people feel rejected by your distance. In the end they feel rejected by you, and you feel rejected by them because they didn't come to chase you as you were pulling away from them. The fear of rejection then becomes a self-fulfilling prophecy, which was the goal of this divisive tormenting spirit all along. It creates a vicious cycle of chaos and torment, seeking to keep you isolated and alone. It needs to be exposed for the dirty villain it actually is. Don't let it hide behind your pain and keep you in torment.

"For if our heart condemns us, God is greater than our heart, and knows all things. Beloved, if our heart does not condemn us, we have confidence toward God" (1 John 3:20-21).

Self-pity also seeks to hide behind traumatic experiences. Yes, self-pity is also a demon, a demon that creates a script that becomes a habit of your flesh, a way of thinking that allows the demonic to have access to your mind and heart. The narrative of self-pity would want you to believe, "It is understandable that I should feel this way, act this way, be stuck in this place, and I have permission to not heal because of what has happened in my life." Trauma is not the only place a demon of self-pity would seek to attach itself, but we want to uncover and expose this nasty demon for his tactics that keep people bound in the most painful places of their history. We don't want to highlight self-pity to bring attention to the Enemy. Instead, we long to reveal this weapon he uses so that you don't fall victim to it.

There **is** an appropriate season of grief attached to loss, pain, or trauma in our lives. The timing of these seasons are relative to the timing of the Holy Spirit in that individual. There is an understandable period of time when you might feel deep sadness over distressing things that have happened, but eventually, that season must come to an end. There is comfort, even during that time period, in knowing that sadness and deep grief won't last forever. The Word of God talks about this in Ecclesiastes 3:4, *"A time to weep and a time to laugh, a time to mourn and a time to dance."* God says there is a time for these things. He understands that we have to process. He understands that we have to rest and rely on him. He understands our heartbreak.

The Enemy wants you to believe there is no rest for your soul. Self-pity wants to come in and help you with that by making sure you constantly remember your pain. Self-Pity moves in when mourning over any loss has passed the appropriate season, and you have stayed in a delayed place where difficult life experiences get so much of your attention that they become intrusive and all-consuming. We want to be sensitive to those mourning the loss of a loved one. We are not talking about the normal twinges of sadness that may come from time to time on special days or events. We are addressing the delayed meditation on any loss that begins to take normal grieving and turn it into torment. Loss is anything that didn't turn out the way you wanted it to or hoped it would.

The demon of self-pity tries to keep you in a place of perpetual hopelessness. It also feeds on the negative attention it receives from having been active in causing pain in a person's life. Self-pity gets a reward when you crave an unholy amount of attention because of what happened in your life during a distressing event. The demon loves it. He wants all the attention to be on the distressing event, not on what the Lord can and has done to offer healing. God offers a way of rest and relief out of the pain and into wholeness.

The Devil loves a good party, and self-pity is the host that never wants the party to end. Pity parties are a real deal. Self-pity will sit at the table and listen to you tell your story over and over and over again. He loves all the details and will actually assist you in remembering all of them. Have you ever thought about how he knows your story so well that he can use it against you? Any time we rehearse or rehash our negative story to ourselves or to others, without the presence of hope or acknowledgment of God's ability to rescue us, we are feeding the unholy hunger of the demonic. Self-pity is drawn to painful stories, and when one is being vocalized without a seed of hope attached to it, he sends out his pity party invitation. Remember, *"The things that come out of a person's mouth come from the heart, and these defile them"* (Matthew 15:18 NIV).

If the demon of self-pity had a bumper sticker, it would read. "No one is here for me, so I must be here for myself. No one understands. I'm all alone." This sticker is intended to become a label that never leaves your mind. As a result, you no longer see people, or even Jesus, as a means to get healthy, and that actually causes your inner sickness to get worse. You push the solution away instead of the pain. You become standoffish to voices of positivity. Preferential treatment is given to holding your pain like a babe in arms, and you are its primary caregiver, as though you cradling it can soothe its never ceasing cries for attention. The demon of self-pity wants you to use your pain narrative as a security blanket because he knows as long as you hold onto it, through the inability to forget, you can't take hold of the hand of Jesus to lift you out of that vicious pit of self-defeat and into His comfort and supernatural justice.

One indicator of a spirit of self-pity is when you feel like you're always crying for help, but nothing offered to you as a solution is ever a viable option. No counsel you receive is ever good enough. There is never a door that says "exit" that you feel like you can take. Nothing is ever enough. **There is a perpetual need to be rescued but a perpetual rejection of the rescue.** You are always in a place of crisis, always wanting to talk and vent, but never wanting to do anything to heal.

Please understand that what we are NOT saying is, "Gloss over the trauma and pain in your life; otherwise, you are partnering with self-pity." On the contrary, the whole point of this book is to minister to the deep places of pain and trauma you may have experienced. We implore you to please not interpret our words in that way. Anywhere trauma has been present, comfort and compassion need to come in and minister to you.

What we are saying is that if a demon of self-pity is holding those painful places hostage, it is a territorial demon that wants to take those places captive as its own. It is like a prison guard who is keeping you locked up in prison to ensure you never get out. It possesses your circumstance, participates in what is causing pain, and wants to daily make you experience that pain over and over again. Self-pity also accuses the Blood of Christ of not being enough to heal the circumstances.

Engaging with a spirit of self-pity is a form of self-comfort. The scheme of self-pity is to keep the compassion and love of the Holy Spirit from having access to bring actual healing and resolve. Self-pity's access point is the need for comfort, but only God has peace, healing, resolve, and true comfort for you.

There is no security in pain, only a fractured ideology that came to life by our disconnect from the power of forgetfulness.

Pain is pleasurable for some people. If you gain attention from being in pain, or if you get permission not to show up in life due to painful experiences, that can be pleasurable. When we experience pleasure, our brain releases dopamine. **We bond to whatever it is that causes us pleasure**, and your brain will actually begin to participate in the demonic attack. This is where your flesh and the Enemy begin to collide. When your brain has now been trained to associate pleasure with pain, the Enemy has come in and attached himself to it, and now you have a real problem because your brain is in agreement that pain is pleasurable. Pain begins offering dopamine, and you are emotionally bonded to your circumstances. You can be bonded to a spirit of self-pity or any other pain-poking demons. If our brain has connected to the idea that it is pleasurable to be in pain because it affords false comfort, gives us attention, causes other people to be responsible for caring for us more than what would normally be healthy, and has learned to settle for a false sense of nurture from being in a perpetual state of crisis, we can stay constantly stuck.

We have to break any agreement that says pain and crisis are pleasurable. You may think, "Oh my goodness, I do not believe that!" You might not think you agree with that, but are you fully fighting for your freedom? Are you more invested in maintaining your painful position, or are you more interested in following the One who can actually set you free? If you do not believe that Jesus Christ is the solution for whatever your circumstance is, you may be in agreement with the culture of, "Pain is pleasurable." You may be in a bonded relationship with self-pity.

The ultimate goal of self-pity is to lead a person to suicide. The final goal of the Enemy is to see a person lose their life without coming to the saving knowledge of Jesus Christ. Satan's goal is for hopelessness to have the final word. Suicide is sneaky and presents itself as a fantasy of escape. It begins as inner dialogue in the first person; it sounds like your own voice speaking to you, offering an escape from pain. Do not be deceived! It is a demon seeking to whisper words of suicidal ideation in your ears for so long that you begin to think in those patterns on your own. This demonic tactic wants to build a stronghold in your mind assuring you that you will always have suicide as an option. This is a nasty scheme of the devil to take your pain and make it feel inescapable, permanent, and hopeless. Suicide is not merciful. Suicide is not an escape. Suicide is the Enemy's plan fully developed and accomplished.

You must not entertain thoughts from a demon of suicide. You must not! Suicide is running to the one who created your pain – the Devil—and expecting him to save you. It is not an option, no matter what has happened. Jesus Christ is your rescuer. Jesus Christ is your Savior. Jesus Christ is the answer to your pain. He is the Healer. He is the Comforter. He is the Prince of Peace. Just because you may not be able to see your way out when you are in deep pain, doesn't mean He isn't real. You have to make a commitment in your own heart that you will never think of suicide as an option.

The trauma you have experienced is not okay with God. He didn't sit by passively and allow the situations that wounded you to occur with His agreement. We know this is a struggle for many people. If God is so good, then why do bad things happen? If God is so loving and powerful, why is my life a cacophony of hardships, disappointment, losses, and turmoil?

The temptation to ask this question is understandable if you turn to look over the landscape of your life and feel like you're looking at a battleground after a war that seems like wreckage everywhere with no mercy in sight. May we ask a question as well, though? In your assessment of God's goodness based on the evidence of your life, does your evaluation also include the very real presence of the devil? Does he bear any weight of responsibility for the hardships you have faced? Do you have an understanding that there is an enemy of your soul whose entire strategy for your life is to kill, steal, and destroy you (John 10:10)? If we evaluate God's goodness based on the evidence of our life thus far, without factoring in the Enemy, we are lacking a significant portion of the equation. That would be like blaming your spouse because someone broke into your house and destroyed everything while you were out to dinner together. Not to be offensive, but that thinking is absurd, even if it is rampant in our culture.

In your assessment of God's power and ability, do you factor in the human will? Do you consider the reality that God gave us human will so that we would be free to choose to be loved by Him and to love Him rather than being created as robots with no choice? God chose to humble Himself and limit His use of power in our lives so that it flows through our agreement with Him. Jesus is a gentleman; He respects your resistance of Him and will not violate your will by forcing Himself where He is not invited. When you are wondering why He hasn't come through in your life the way you may have expected Him to, ask yourself, "Did I allow Him?

Was He invited? Was He invited into the lives of the people who hurt me?" He is not responsible for behaviors instigated by the Enemy. The Enemy needs to be held responsible for attacks he has launched at our lives in an effort to destroy us, not the Lord.

We have to make sure we have all the players accounted for before we assign blame for our circumstances. The other half of John 10:10 talks about God's desire for you to have life and have it in abundance! Which side of the John 10:10 Scripture are you living in agreement with? Anyone who has intentionally wounded you has been aligning himself with the Enemy, and the Enemy should be held responsible for his actions. We can't blame God for humans walking in their flesh or the Enemy being a thief, a killer, and a destroyer. Jesus, on the other hand, laid down His life to make a way for you to heal from a wound that He didn't cause. His answer to your devastation is to point you toward Heaven, which is pure intimacy with your Father and an infinity of joy in the home He built for you.

Your eternity was **meant** to be spent in Heaven, even if what you have encountered in your life on earth feels like hellish circumstances. Shame, rejection, self-pity, and suicide are not meant to have any place in your life. You were born for Heaven. You were born for love and to experience the tangible goodness of God for all of eternity. Don't you dare give up on God! Don't you dare settle! Don't you dare let the Enemy have the last word!

In the next few chapters, we are going to help walk you through solutions that will overcome these strategies of the Enemy. You are not alone. You are cherished by God. You are worth fighting for. You have to fight for yourself, and you have to let the Lord fight on your behalf. You have to press in no matter what it takes. You have to believe that not only can you be free, but your freedom was won a long time ago on the cross! Jesus wants you to step into His healing path and walk all the way through to the other side, all the way to the freedom His sacrificed life affords you. Your freedom is the treasure He purchased with His precious Blood. Remember the zit imagery? Well, Jesus is coming back for a Bride who is holy and without blemish (Ephesians 5:27); and that includes you. You are meant to be part of the Bride of Christ, fully cleansed, fully healed, fully holy, and without blemish. See, Friend, that zit reference was holy the whole time!

Don't give the Enemy, and any lethal weapon of his, permission to edit the glorious biography of your life by putting periods to any sentences, rewriting any chapters, or revising where the ending is. Your life's manuscript originated from the heart of a loving, faithful, all-powerful Father who invested His great love, Jesus, to ensure the success of your life and its story. Beloved, one day, Jesus will tell your story to all of heaven. It is to be a love story in the midst of a battle, where you are a valiant warrior who cuts down every foe, every time. Jesus believes in you! The son of God is on your side, championing your every moment of faith in Him. You are not alone in this fight for your abundant life. Jesus is with you. Never forget you are called victorious, overcomer, and conqueror for a reason. These are words describing the outcome of war, deliberate words of your identity that point to the other side of perilous times. Do you see the punctuation mark?

This is how your story ends. This is the glorious unfolding of who you are!

The Enemy shakes in his scales at the thought of you ever connecting to how powerful you are against him. The Enemy and all his horde know if you catch the fire, from having looked from the end of your story first, you'll start slicing him with your sword of truth, and he'll never get a word in edge-wise! This, this is the place where your story gets really good. Warrior of God, you will tell your testimonies to everyone you know who needs its encouragement. Why would the enemy want to mess with you? Because you, your faith, your victory, you taking him by force could equate to thousands of people never feeling the heat of battle the way you did because you opened their eyes to a battle strategy that ended their war before it ever began. So, tell your story. We implore you to tell everyone you know everything. Just don't forget to tell them about how you know the end of your story, no matter what side of the story you may be on right now. Slice, pow, kaboom. There it is. That's the sound of faith, and it's truth bombs.

"I have told all your people about your justice. I have not been afraid to speak out, as you, O Lord, well know. I have not kept the good news of your justice hidden in my heart; I have talked about your faithfulness and saving power. I have told everyone in the great assembly of your unfailing love and faithfulness" (Psalm 40:9-10, NLT).

CHAPTER EIGHT

COMFORT

Whew! That last chapter was a doozy. For those who read straight through chapter Seven, put down your sword and let us take a breath together, shall we? Breathe in through your nose, "one, two, three," and out your mouth, "one, two, three, four, five, six, seven." Excellent. Did you know it helps to relieve stress when you breathe out longer than you breathe in? This chapter will be a breath of fresh air compared to the last one. Promise.

Perhaps we should start with something a little more lighthearted. How about a game? That's an idea! Okay. Have you ever played the word association game? It's often used as an icebreaker because it's a fun way to get to know people. One person says a word, and everyone goes in a circle to share the first thing that word makes them think of—word association. Let's play.

What is the first thing you think of in association with the word *blue*?

How about the word *exit*?

This is the last one. Are you ready? What is the first thing you think about with the word *comfort*?

Did you think of something? Good job.

"Pajamas!" That is my (Amber's) random response. I saw myself running to my suitcase after a fiery day of slicing devils with our ministry team, Contagious Love. In less than five minutes, I had fashioned myself in my comfy cozies (aka pajamas). Ahh! The relief. If you know me, I know you are having a good chuckle. If you do not know me, but you can relate, can I get an amen?

The first word that pops into my (Rachel's) mind is hugs; however, pajamas are a close second. If I had to choose between the two, then cozy, snuggly, warm hugs win out in my heart. Kind of like Olaf, I love warm hugs. I especially love hugging on my kiddos, my hubby, and my puppies. Hugs are a wonderfully perfect gift; you give and receive at the same time. It's not selfish; it just so happens that the more you give, the more you receive. What a wonderful notion.

What were the words, thoughts, images, or emotions you felt when you read the word *comfort*?

Does it seem challenging to even connect with that word at all?

The word association game is actually rather revealing because the connection to the idea of comfort is relative to your understanding. What specifically prompts your desire for comfort? Your answer to that question helps you determine where you think comfort is warranted and where it is not. What do you find comforting? The things you welcome as comforting can reveal the level of value you place on yourself. Do you allow yourself to feel comforted? Do you despise the need for comfort? For some people, the need for comfort is a source of pain because it triggers the memory of needing comfort while finding none. **Detachment from comfort is often a scar related to trauma.**

The very nature of comfort is that you need it most when you feel uncomfortable. The more uncomfortable you feel, the more you long to be comforted. That longing becomes an ache, and if the need for comfort isn't met, the ache becomes increasingly painful.

It is unfathomable to think that there are precious hearts starving for comfort, but their brains do not even know how to compute the concept. It is innate within us to need comfort. Never experiencing comfort would be absolutely tormenting. To know that there are some wounded hearts that haven't had access to comfort or cannot even imagine how to receive the experience of comfort is heartbreaking. Friend, if that is you, please know that we have prayed over you for the very moment you read these words, and we want you to know that comfort is coming. Our hearts are with you, and more importantly, Jesus' heart is right there with you.

Your worldview is powerful, and everyone's perception is based on his or her life's education. We (Amber and Rachel) both have friends who would vehemently disagree that pajamas are even in the category of comfort. Both friends had a lengthy season of physical illness where all they did was lie in bed with pajamas on, fighting to regain their health. If we had their experience, we might change our minds about pajamas too. This is important to grasp because if we do not understand that our perception of comfort can be completely different than someone else's, we may limit receptibility and may falter in our accuracy as we try to comfort others. Just because you dive into half a gallon of ice cream to soothe your broken heart does not mean that it will help your lactose-intolerant friend.

All manner of things can be seen as options for comfort: french fries, burgers, ice cream, candy, mashed potatoes, warm bread, chocolate… I mean, we do call them comfort foods. Bubble baths, candles, spa treatments, shopping trips…yes, please, and thank you. We would also be remiss not to mention the sinful comforts we reach for when chocolate cake and the like are not enough, things like gambling, shoplifting, drugs, alcohol, promiscuity, and all manner of sexual perversion. This world is a convenience store of options.

What is it that we are really after in the moments we long for comfort?? In simple terms, we want to stop feeling uncomfortable, right? We want to lessen the stress, pain, and grief, as well as the awareness of our discomfort.

In our current culture, "comfort" has shifted its definition to include whatever immediately appeals to you at the moment that will ease your discomfort. Even if the source of comfort is unhealthy, the world says, "If you want it, go for it." What we may or may not realize when we act on this shallow attempt at attaining comfort is that, in so doing, we have aligned our will against the very source of true comfort. Our need for comfort is actually a holy desire. It is meant to be a place of connection with God.

Think about the cry of a newborn infant when he is hungry. It isn't only physical nourishment that he receives when his mother offers her milk supply to satisfy the hunger of his little belly. God designed this beautiful method of nourishment because it is also meant to provide nurture and comfort. A child's hunger cry cue and the loving responses of mothers and fathers are meant to shape our worldview with the understanding that when we have a need, it will be met not only with nourishment but also with comfort, when we receive it from the intended source. Our God-designed needs are meant to lead us to Him.

When we reach for comfort from a lesser source than what God intended, it is like giving a hungry baby a pacifier. It may quiet the cries for a moment, but it certainly won't satisfy; it has no power to do so, and the hunger will only ever increase. Reaching for worldly pacifiers expresses to God our inability to see that His involvement is necessary or preferred.

Most of us would not consciously say, "Lord, I do not want your comfort." But if we stop to examine our lives, will we find that we indirectly say this to Him more often than we realize? When our comfort levels are no longer tolerable and needs begin to ache within us, what are we reaching for most often? When we binge a tv series that has the most veg potential, or scarf down our favorite pasta dish for the third time this week, or scroll social media to distract our minds and ignore the need entirely, we are employing self-comfort (self-help). When we reach for things to satisfy our flesh in the immediate, in our own efforts, according to our own reasoning, we are reaching for pacifiers. Self-comfort actually delays the solution to our needs and compounds the discomfort.

What we don't want you to hear is that you cannot eat a piece of chocolate or enjoy a soak in the hot tub after an unpleasant day. We are not saying that you shouldn't reach for your pajamas or a hug from your spouse when you feel the need for comfort. In fact, God created so much of what exists as a healthy source of pleasure or comfort.

Ecclesiastes 9:7 tells us, *"Go eat your food and enjoy it,"* so it isn't that natural sources of comfort are inherently bad. No, but we can easily abuse what was meant for good in our efforts to find a measure of permanent comfort that only God can fill. The question is, how loud is your ache for comfort? How deep does it go? Is it really just about a long day? We know what it feels like to have an exhausting weekend of traveling, working, and pouring yourself out until you feel beyond tired, and comfort is all your body is asking for. But after a hot shower, a home-cooked meal, a pair of clean, cozy pajamas, and a really good night's sleep in your own bed, is the ache for comfort still crying out at a pretty high volume? Dear One, that cry matters.

Not every uncomfortable thing we face requires a miracle. But sometimes. Sometimes there is something deeper going on inside, and we aren't willing to pay attention to it. We push it away. We deny it. We ignore the cry. Perhaps that is because deep down, we don't know what to do with it. We don't know how to satisfy it, quiet it, or just make it stop. What we are asking you to ponder is, "Are you perpetually self-soothing? Has your need for your choice of comfort gone beyond a moment that passes and become a lifestyle of reaching for something to help you feel better?

When you are longing for reprieve from what happened in your life, is Heaven invited in?

The problem behind all the solutions we offer ourselves is that they fail to comfort us as we hope they will. What is really happening in that steamy tub is that the edge is being taken off. You are less uncomfortable because your nervous system is being calmed as serotonin is released. What we need to understand, though, is that even though our serotonin levels are increasing, the deep need at the root of the situation is still there, just as present. The need will lay dormant, but it will never be fully silenced, never satisfied. Human efforts cannot aid what was intended for Holy intervention.

There is a difference between our efforts to attain comfort and a touch from The Comforter.

The Holy Spirit is the Comforter. To dive deep into the sweetness of Him is exponentially, eternally more satisfying than anything this world can offer. Do you know Him? Have you invited Him fully into your spirit? Have you asked Jesus to baptize you into the Holy Spirit?

"He who sent me to baptize with water said to me, 'Upon whom you see the Spirit descending, and remaining on Him, this is He who baptizes with the Holy Spirit'" (John 1:33).

Jesus saves our souls, and then in His audacious love, He offers to baptize us into His Holy Spirit. That is unfathomable generosity. It is unimaginable kindness. It is infinite love. He is unending, unrelenting comfort. Have you partaken of this love feast offering? Jesus Himself is the Baptizer. You can simply ask Him, in faith, for this incredible gift of more of Him. If you have not done so, you can, right where you are. Ask Him, "Jesus, I have given my heart to you. I have accepted your sacrificial gift of love that offers me salvation. And now, my heart is hungry for more of You even still. Will you please baptize me with the Holy Spirit?" Pause and give Him an opportunity to respond to your request. He knows just how to minister to you at this moment.

If you just asked to be baptized with the Holy Spirit for the first time, welcome into the sweetest waters you will ever swim in and the deepest experience of love you have ever known. Pay attention to your spirit, and expect Him to make Himself known in a greater capacity. The more you yield to Him and partner with Him, the better and better it gets.

The Holy Spirit is the Comforter. He is the Helper.

"Nevertheless I tell you the truth. It is to your advantage that I go away; for if I do not go away, the Helper will not come to you; but if I depart, I will send Him to you" (John 16:7).

Do you see the connection between Jesus and the Holy Spirit in this passage? Jesus had to go away so that the Spirit could come. He wanted the Helper, the Comforter, to be able to minister at a greater capacity than He could while He was one man walking the earth. He wanted His Spirit to be able to move at a much greater capacity than the limitations of being bound in the flesh. Remember that Jesus is fully God, but He also humbled Himself to be fully man as well. The flesh had to be separated to make room for the Spirit. To relate to Him, we must also be in our spirits and not in our flesh.

Jesus wanted the Holy Spirit to have the boundless capacity to comfort our souls. He is not intimidated by the depth of our needs, no matter how deep of an abyss they may feel like to us. The Holy Spirit knows every place in our hearts. He knows every memory, every moment, every circumstance, every breath we have taken, every word we have spoken, and everything that has happened during every millisecond of our lives. He knows us infinitely better than we could even know ourselves. Do you realize that? He already knows! Read the words of King David in Psalm 139 and let them remind your heart how deeply God knows you and loves you.

Beloved, the Comforter is here for you. He was there for you in the past, and he is here for you in the present. He will be there for you in the future. Every time you ask the Comforter to help, He answers. That is a promise.

We must learn *how* to connect to the Comforter and *how* to receive from Him. We can easily miss His presence, His direction, and His offerings of comfort if we don't know what to look for. We won't understand His expressions through our natural interpretations. We can miss a transformative encounter with our Comforter if we aren't looking through the lens of our spirit. You see, Dear One, we must travel much higher than this earthen realm and our earthly vessel to grasp His greatness. His comfort is supernatural.

"But the natural man does not receive the things of the Spirit of God, for they are foolishness to him; nor can he know them, because they are spiritually discerned" (1 Corinthians 2:14).

To see how the Comforter enters into our need, our lens must be rinsed of a worldly view and must align with Heaven's view. We are fully equipped, but only through our spirit can we receive the Holy Spirit. If we are waiting for the Comforter to feel like earthly comfort, we not only limit His power to shift our atmosphere, but we also shut down His capacity to reward our trust in Him.

How do we see Him? How do we connect to Him from a heavenly perspective, from our spirit?

We lean into the wisdom of the Word to guide us into all comfort, through the leading of the Comforter Himself. Jesus is the Word (John 1:1), and He went to the Father so that we could receive the blessing of the Holy Spirit.

He has a vested interest in teaching us how to connect with the Holy Spirit, so He tucked away some instructions in His Word.

We can connect with the Holy Spirit by accepting the truth that He is near to us when we are brokenhearted. *"The LORD is near to the brokenhearted and saves the crushed in spirit"* (Psalm 34:18).

If your children were brokenhearted, wouldn't you draw close to them, hold them, and comfort them? Imagine how a mother or father would run to the rescue of their hurting child. This is how the Comforter feels about you. He wants you to feel His nearness and sense His presence, especially when you are hurting. You can connect to Him by meditating on that thought. Where am I hurting? If I picture the Comforter holding me in that place of pain, what would that feel like?

"Blessed be the God and Father of our Lord Jesus Christ, the Father of mercies and God of all comfort, who comforts us in all our affliction, so that we may be able to comfort those who are in any affliction, with the comfort with which we ourselves are comforted by God" (2 Corinthians 1:3-4).

The Holy Spirit offers us comfort by strengthening us in our inner being. He saves the crushed in spirit and wants to strengthen their inner being. Where is your inner being, your spirit, your heart, your soul? It is comforting to know that He wants to strengthen you with His power.

"That He would grant you, according to the riches of His glory, to be strengthened with might through his Spirit in your inner man" (Ephesians 3:16).

Beloved, He is not asking you to strengthen yourself with your own power. He is not saying that you should buck up, pick yourself up by the bootstraps, and move on. He is saying, "Listen, My precious child, I know you are hurting and in need of comfort. Can I please be the One to strengthen you by My Spirit and My power, all according to My riches and glory?" Not sure what your glory and riches bank account looks like, but it is hard to imagine anyone feeling like what they are working with is greater in value than God's riches and glory! Strength is what is being offered to you, and comfort through being strengthened in the very places you feel crushed in spirit. That is what comfort looks like through a heavenly perspective—nearness, strengthening, and relief in affliction.

He also comforts with truth. This is the place where we can often be tempted to pull away. His comfort isn't always comfortable, but it is always good and always for our ultimate benefit. Comfort through truth results in peace in the places that felt like they were in torment.

"When the Spirit of truth has come, He will guide you into all truth; for He will not speak on His own authority, but whatever He hears, He will speak..." (John 16:13).

Truth leads to understanding, and understanding leads to peace. We cannot shut down our willingness to receive the revelation of truth from the Holy Spirit and expect to feel any lasting comfort. Truth can feel confronting, but it can also feel like a surgeon's knife is cutting into the depths of our pain. Usually, this is the very thing that is necessary because the Enemy's lies, embedded in our thoughts, are causing us to be in so much tormenting pain in the first place. Where there has been trauma, the Enemy has been present. Until we allow the skillful, merciful hand of the Comforter to come in and expose lies with the purity of the truth, we will stay in a suffering state. God's truth is not condemning; It is liberating. When we come to a place of understanding, we have encountered the Holy Spirit, the Comforter.

Many years ago, the Lord gave me (Amber) the opportunity to walk a healing journey with a man who had been sexually abused by his third-grade teacher. His trauma, like so many others who have experienced similar tragedies, was marked by many different emotions and responses. He felt humiliation, shame, anger, grief, and self-loathing. He also felt great guilt and responsibility for what had been perpetrated against him, and this sense of guilt prompted him to keep his painful trauma a secret.

Even as an adult, knowing it wasn't his fault, it felt impossible for him to reconcile the situation any differently. The same feelings that kept this tragedy hidden for decades had created a cycle of suffering and self-comfort that led to addiction and secrets that were destroying his personal life and family. In his bravery to confront the pain by finally revealing the truth, the Holy Spirit began a healing process that ultimately brought true comfort.

Bringing things into the light of truth invited the miracle-working power of the Holy Spirit to bring redemption. His family was restored, demons of addiction were cast out, and the torment from sinful desires and patterns was instantly gone. Miraculous! However, it took more than one prayer for this precious man to experience delivery from pain and for unhealthy brain patterns to rewire. We walked this healing journey together as comfort came in wave after wave for nearly three years. The Lord patiently revealed layer upon layer of lies that the Enemy had forged into his thinking, belief systems about the injustice of life, himself, and even his view of God. It took this dear brother so long to walk out this process, not because he wasn't interested in immediate healing, but because the wisdom of God knew his heart needed that much time. God knew there was only so much his precious heart could bear all at once.

His journey with the Comforter wasn't always easy, and often it was painfully uncomfortable. I can remember many times, as the Lord would reveal a hidden layer, his response would be, "THERE'S MORE?? HOW LONG IS THIS GOING TO TAKE?!" But in obedience, he would press in for more from the Holy Spirit, and the strongholds of the devil's delusions would be confronted. Each and every time, he would have a "light bulb" moment as truth overcame the lies, one more weight lifted from his soul, one more neural pathway was healed, and peace came to another of his pieces. If we spoke to him today, he would probably tell you he is still being comforted by the refining fire of the Holy Spirit.

"Now may the God of hope fill you with all joy and peace in believing, that you may abound in hope by the power of the Holy Spirit" (Romans 15:13). You know you have experienced the Comforter when you feel refreshing waves of peace, joy, hope, love, and all the fruit of the Spirit.

"But the fruit produced by the Holy Spirit within you is divine love in all its varied expressions: joy that overflows, peace that subdues, patience that endures, kindness in action, a life full of virtue, faith that prevails, gentleness of heart, and strength of spirit" (Galatians 5:22 TPT).

When you want to feel the comfort of the Comforter, you look for the evidence of His presence. When you encounter His fruit, you encounter the Comforter. This also means that when you experience the fruit of the Spirit through the life of another spirit-filled believer, you have been embraced by the Comforter Himself.

The Holy Spirit binds up broken hearts. He declares freedom to captive people. He rescues us out of our prisons. He comforts those who mourn and makes beautiful the places that were in an ash heap (Isaiah 61). His heart is for us, and His love is immeasurable.

Engaging with the comfort of the Comforter is the very pathway to healing. Every time we yield and allow the Holy Spirit into our needs, our brain's reward system is being activated.

"But without faith it is impossible to please Him, for he who comes to God must believe that He is, and that He is a rewarder of those who diligently seek Him" (Hebrews 11:6).

Did you know that our every encounter with the Comforter floods our bodies with pleasure chemicals? It is true. Our Father in Heaven designed our brains to absolutely overflow with pleasure chemicals when we connect with the Comforter. He did this on purpose because He loves us so.

Oxytocin, serotonin, dopamine, and endorphins are all pleasure chemicals. They are released by the brain in many different circumstances. They are the chemicals that affect how we feel. They can help us feel love, friendship, and deep trust. We can experience these pleasure chemicals with many kinds of things, including physical touch, chocolate, and exercise. Even as mamas are nursing their babies, these chemicals are being released. Drugs, alcohol, and sexual perversions also offer a fraudulent option if we choose to abuse our bodies with sin.

Ideally, we can feel the release of these pleasure chemicals through prayer and connection with God. Oxytocin and serotonin, the love and mood chemicals, are released through prayer, connection, giving, messages of love, and warm hugs. Dopamine and endorphins, the happy, feel-good chemicals, are released through rest, worship, dancing, intimacy, and laughter. All of these beautiful substances are created by God to be released in our brains during activities that bond us to HIM. This is what our brain is doing when we relate to Him. He IS our greatest source of pleasure. Pleasure was His idea and by His design, for our comfort and well-being.

"Because of you, I know the path of life, as I taste the fullness of joy in your presence. At your right side I experience divine pleasures forevermore!" (Psalm 16:11).

The Holy Spirit is the revealer of our hearts, mind, and emotions. He is the greatest life highlighter; however, if you feel uncomfortable as He begins to move on your behalf, you may reject His assistance by not understanding that He is the One moving in your heart. Remember world view? When the Holy Spirit offers truth that goes against our worldview, it may feel uncomfortable to our flesh, and understandably so. But we must learn how to flow from our spirit in regards to the tribulations of our past, present, and future. Every difficulty is an opportunity for this transition. His fiery love burns hot, and every place that hurts you is on the table.

The Holy Spirit is our Advocate, Helper, Counselor, Paraclete (one who is called alongside, one who intercedes on our behalf), and COMFORTER. When we have ongoing issues of the heart, mind, and soul (places where trauma has rendered us incapacitated), only He can come alongside us and offer us lasting change. Nothing available in this world will ever be able to take His intended place in our lives. His presence is not only a partnership but a relationship. **There is great hope in the truth that we are not alone.** We cannot express this enough. Those words sound simple, but they are profoundly accurate. The absolute best of Heaven literally resides within you.

Our bodies are the temple of the Holy Spirit, the outer court, the inner court, and the Holy of Holies. Never forget that the day that Jesus was crucified, the earth trembled and shook, and the veil that separated the Holy of Holies was torn down. Today, the Presence that was purposefully confined to a single small room has been unleashed to fill the whole temple. Beloved, we are the temple His Spirit has filled! The Comforter is here IN you! He longs to walk with you, talk with you, sit with you, and be there to wipe every one of your tears. Within the small spaces of your being, His transcendent glory pulses with every beat of your heart.

Beloved, spiritual senses can translate into natural experiences. Every moment of clarity, whoosh of peace, and sudden shift into truth, is Him. Recollections of things long forgotten that offer understanding to your mind, soul, or body are also Him. Every epiphany that brings peace and rest is the fruit that proves you have been supernaturally embraced by The Comforter.

"Daily I will worship you passionately and with all my heart. My arms will wave to you like banners of praise. I overflow with praise when I come before you, for the anointing of your presence satisfies me like nothing else. You are such a rich banquet of pleasure to my soul" (Psalm 63:4-5 TPT).

Can you feel the supernatural comfort of the Holy Spirit? You will if you allow Him in. He will bathe you in His love, shower you with His wisdom, kiss you with His mercy and truth, and embrace you with His gentle kindness. Every encounter with him is a feast for your hungry soul. The table is set. Are you ready to partake?

CHAPTER NINE

HEALING

Where are you sitting as you read this? If you are in a chair, on a couch, or in a place where you can stand up and do an exercise, let's do this next part together. If you're on a plane or sitting in a coffee shop… well, we can still do this together. You might get some looks from the people around you; but hey, you can teach them what you learn on the other side of it. You'll need to stand to your feet. Put your feet shoulder length apart. Now, raise your arms above your head in a "V" shape. Put your head back, and look to the ceiling. Hold this position for sixty seconds.

Seriously. Try it.

Did you hold it for the whole sixty seconds?

Okay, if you didn't actually do the exercise yet, you will want to when you learn about what could happen to your brain. If you actually did it, here is what just happened. You just told your brain that you won something. Right now, your brain is releasing the chemicals of victory throughout your entire body. Isn't that amazing? You just told your body that you are a winner. Your brain was actually taught to associate this posture with victory as you were growing up. Think about the victory stance parents use when they cheer for their babies as they learn to walk, do something especially great, or in celebration of a victory. Runners take this pose as they cross the finish line in a race. Athletes celebrate a win with this same posture. Our brains have been taught that this is a universal sign that means victory.

Did you know that the victory stance started back before the world began? It actually started with our Heavenly Father. Think about the posture of worship: our hands raised, our heads back, and our eyes on Jesus. He prompted the victory response, and He is the One most worthy of that stance. In Christ, we also become victorious because God says we are! Through the power of God, we become overcomers and conquerors. That is who we are, not just something we can do. It is part of our spiritual identity, and we need to claim that.

This is actually an exercise that is utilized by professionals who train people how to succeed in job opportunities. They encourage people to go into any available space, and stay in this stance for at least one minute, and then they automatically perform better in the interview process. This is because their brain has been switched into a gear that says, "I can! I am enough, and you need me!"

Our brains are impressionable. This reality may have caused us some damage to our brains through trauma when we were younger, but it additionally holds within its truth a great deal of hope. It means our brain can be influenced into a mindset of victory, as well. Most importantly, it means our brains have the ability to change. That is amazing news!

For decades, doctors believed trauma was permanent damage to the brain. It wasn't until the late eighties that this belief began to be challenged and explored in the medical community. Trauma presented itself as untreatable, irreversible damage to the brain tissue. Damage from trauma can be visibly seen on scanned images of the brain. What a defeating perspective to think it is permanent, but the research that has been done over the past three decades shows those findings to be inaccurate. Our brains can, in fact, heal. There is now so much scientific proof of this, even from the medical community.

Did you catch that? Our brains can heal! The damage done to our brains from trauma can heal!

By the design of God, the brain is malleable. It is impressionable, pliable, and teachable. No matter what you have experienced, no matter how long ago you have experienced something difficult, no matter how tragic, big or small, the brain can be taught to change its mind. This incredible reset is called neuroplasticity. Neuroplasticity is the ability of neural networks in the brain to change through growth and reorganization. Your brain can be rewired to function in a way that differs from how it previously functioned. Isn't that amazing?

Your brain is waiting for you to teach it something new, and it will adapt to this new way of connecting by releasing the previous education and replacing it with the new one. You literally get to stand in the position of educator over your mind, your thoughts, and your history. You may not have caused what happened in your life, and you may not have initiated the distressing event(s), but you can help retrain your brain to reprocess. That means that you have a tremendous amount of influence over your healing journey.

This healing, the reeducating of your brain, includes the opportunity for your nervous system to no longer control your emotions based on previous trauma-related stimuli. Your emotions can change. Your nervous system can heal. Those evocative cues and the way that you respond to them can shift. You can feel differently as you learn to connect differently with your history.

Romans 12:2 says, *"Be transformed by the renewing of your mind."* God knows what He is talking about in this verse. He means it when He says there is hope for our transformation! How do we access this healing? We have to posture our hearts to look up. The Word says to look up; that is where your help comes from.

"I lift up my eyes to the mountains—where does my help come from? My help comes from the Lord, the Maker of heaven and earth" (Psalm 121:1-2 NIV).

We are meant to flock to God, so, when we look up to the Lord, we are flocking to Him. Did you know that when we look up, those feel-good chemicals in our brain increase? Just the activity of looking up releases the pleasure chemicals to rush through our bodies. It is a drink of refreshment to help our bodies feel better. There is scientific proof behind God's desire to draw our eyes to Him!

We have to posture our hearts to know this is where our help is coming from. We are not teaching you self-help or self-comfort; that is not what this is. What we are teaching you is that God created your brain to be able to reorganize, rewire, and refresh as you look to Him. Eventually, your brain will begin to remind you that when you need comfort and refreshment, you should look up. The chemicals in your body help you to bond with God and create a habit of desiring His presence first when you are in need.

In our last chapter, we talked in depth about the Comforter. He longs to bring peace and rest to our souls. He wants to bring peace to our pieces and wholeness to our hurts. The things that hurt you matter to Him.

You are not broken. Can you say that to yourself, please? "I am not broken!" We can no longer live under the condemnation and shame of wondering what is wrong with us. Have you ever asked yourself the following questions? "What is wrong with me? Why can't I get it together? Why can't I be better at this or that? Why does this have to matter to me?" Friend, it is not that there is something wrong with you; the reality is that something happened to you.

We were not born traumatized. You were not created by God with trauma embedded in your brain and soul. He didn't create you as faulty and broken, nor did He design you to live in the exhaustion of carrying trauma. Something happened to you.

What happened? Where did it start? Where did it come from? These are the types of questions we need to ask instead. Posture your heart in curiosity and compassion rather than judgment, including towards yourself.

If you have suffered trauma, there is loss associated with those events. Trauma's impact can cause you to mourn the loss of whole parts of your life. Your entire childhood may have felt like a collection of losses and pain. Maybe you are mourning the loss of a mother or maybe you grew up without feeling the safety of a mother's love. You can grieve the loss of a loving father who offered safety and protection, or perhaps your father was physically or emotionally absent. You can mourn the loss of a peaceful home, an unviolated body, the loss of innocence, or the loss associated with your parents' divorce or even your own divorce.

You might find yourself mourning the fact that you never had a normal, healthy childhood. Suddenly, you may recognize what was withheld from you as you witness other people experiencing a loving childhood, one you might not have known was even possible. Perhaps no one ever wrote notes that said, "I love you," and put them in your lunch box. You might not have even known that was a thing parents did. It can be traumatizing to see the way your life experiences compare to others.

I (Rachel) remember watching television as a child and having my worldview challenged. Before I was adopted, our family didn't feel like the Cosby's, or Growing Pains, or the old reruns of The Brady Bunch. Until I witnessed something different, I didn't fully realize what could have been. Afterwards, I remember the ache inside as I observed other people experiencing the love of family. It was validating, sobering, and tormenting all at the same time.

Loss is experienced when anything in life doesn't turn out the way it should have.

The Word of God says He will comfort all who mourn. Matthew 5:4 says, *"Blessed are those who mourn, for they will be comforted."*

I (Amber) remember my dad talking about a word study he did on the word mourn. The root of the word mourn holds the idea that those who wait upon God will be comforted. He offers solace to those who wait in the midst of the hard, in the midst of the pain, in the midst of the trauma, disillusionment, confusion, fear, or the unknown. Those who wait upon God, with their face turned towards Him, are those who will experience His comfort.

We need to give ourselves space, time, and margin and wait on Him. We do this knowing that His comfort is available for us right where we are. You were not intended to endure pain. You were not intended to have gaps full of loss in your life. God longs to comfort you.

Healing is not primarily about a power struggle; it is a love encounter.

Anywhere the Enemy has been allowed access, God and His love have not been invited. God will not violate our will in order to dwell in places that have been given to the Enemy. Those places have to be taken back from the Enemy, and God has to be given access in order for us to heal. He has to be given room for His love to wash over those wounds.

Are you ready, beloved of God?

We have sought to bring you to a greater level of understanding about how trauma is developed, how the Enemy targets those places of trauma, and how God desires to bring healing to those traumatized pieces. Let us now posture our hearts to partner with the Comforter as He walks us through the "how" of healing.

We can follow Him down two main paths to healing from trauma. The first pathway to healing is to heal by intention. We can choose to enter into memories and places where we know healing is needed when we are not currently being thrust into a triggered state. You can choose to journey toward healing alone with the Holy Spirit, or partner with the Holy Spirit and a friend or mentor. On this path, you're in control of preparing your heart to face the trauma and memories. The beautiful part of this pathway is that you enter into it with the full awareness of your prefrontal cortex. You are already in a rational state. You are aware of when and where you are. Your emotions are not heightened, and you're not having to come down from an arousal state.

When you enter into your memories from a place of peace, it is easier for your body and your heart to handle. You can also choose to partner with a person you trust as you dip into the memories associated with your trauma.

Proverbs 18:14 says, "*The spirit of a man will sustain him in sickness; But who can bear a broken spirit?*"

We cannot bear the level of pain and agony that comes from carrying trauma. We know we need to come to a place of peace. On the cross, Jesus cried, "It is finished." His suffering can be the end of your suffering. All we have to do is agree with that, and choose to follow Him into healing.

One of the challenges that can keep us from walking into healing is that dealing with our trauma never quite feels desirable or convenient. If you're having a good day, then you may not be experiencing a trigger of any kind. You're busy living your life, and it can feel undesirable to choose to go poking around in your pain closet. We are busy people. Remember the chapter on stress? We have things to do, responsibilities to tend to, and families to care for. It can feel really inconvenient to intentionally visit places of pain when you aren't in a triggered state. That is not really what we would consider a fun way to spend the afternoon, but what we need to keep in mind is the level of exhaustion we are experiencing due to unresolved trauma. Heartbreak that is on a low simmer, in the background of our everyday life, doesn't go away by ignoring it. As a matter of fact, the triggers that are attached to that pain threaten to hijack our day at any given moment. When that happens, we have just lost the fullness of the opportunity to enter that memory from a place of peace.

Avoiding the pain of healing doesn't make your situation better. It keeps you in a place of suffering. It doesn't relieve injustice for you to avoid healing. Not only have you had to endure trauma in the first place, but now you inadvertently end up serving up the rest of your life on a silver platter to the Enemy because you aren't willing to fight back on your own behalf.

Beloved, you cannot stay in a stuck place, thinking, "It is not that bad. I think I can endure a little more. I'm just going to keep avoiding things." You have the opportunity to be intentional by turning and looking at your pain and saying, "You know what? No matter how painful it feels, I am going to face this. I am going to walk through this. The Holy Spirit is going to take me by the hand, and I am willing to look at my past, face it, and walk through the hurt to the other side, no matter how painful it feels."

Consciously choosing to face your pain and walk through to healing is what fighting alongside the Holy Spirit looks like as you grapple for justice against the kingdom of darkness. It takes courage to choose to heal, and you are worth fighting for.

Joshua 1:9 (NIV) says, "*Be strong and courageous. Do not be afraid, do not be discouraged, for God will be with you wherever you go.*"

You have to recognize Jesus' partnership and His willingness to guide you to the other side. You do not need to be afraid to walk out of your pain. He is the anesthetic to your pain. So often, during the revival services we do in our ministry, we watch joy break out. It is literally like watching God dump buckets of joy all over the room. Suddenly, right in the midst of the joy and laughter, He will begin to heal people from trauma. It is like serving pain medicine before a surgery.

He is so kind and gentle. So let's choose to heal. Let's choose to trust Him. Let's choose to believe that He will comfort and soothe us as we face our pain.

The second pathway to healing is by taking advantage of a triggered moment. While it may not be the most desirable pathway, you can absolutely experience healing through a triggered moment.

Triggers are not something to fear, no matter how inconvenient they are. Triggers may be outside of our control and often happen at very inopportune times. They also tend to happen in very inopportune places, maybe even when you are surrounded by people you may not want to be vulnerable with. However, triggered moments can still yield healing and spirit-filled resilience.

The advantage of healing through a trigger is that it functions as a breadcrumb that can lead us right to the root of a traumatic memory. Often when we experience triggers, we don't know what the memory is until we follow the breadcrumb. We might not have been able to enter into a place of healing from a calm, intentional state. It sometimes takes a triggered memory for us to even recognize its presence. So don't be discouraged if the opportunity to heal is being presented to you by the discomfort of a trigger. Rather, take advantage of the information your body is offering you, and let the Holy Spirit bring revelation and understanding to the cause of the trigger.

We know triggers can seem very scary and wildly uncomfortable. May we please tell you how sorry we are if you have ever had to feel one at all? We both have experienced triggers as well, and we know they can actually feel quite horrible.

Be patient and peaceful with yourself; trust the Holy Spirit, and allow Him to lead you. He can turn every trigger into a treasure of healing.

We have these two pathways available for us to heal from trauma. We are going to talk more in the next chapters about how to do that. Whether we get the opportunity to press in for healing from a calm state or take advantage of a triggered moment to press in for healing, the bottom line is that healing can come. God's heart is for us to heal. That is good news. Every place of trauma, every place of pain, and every place of torment is pregnant with the opportunity for an encounter with the powerful, loving attention of your Heavenly Father. When we are willing to allow God to enter into those places with us, we cannot help but be changed. His presence changes everything.

CHAPTER TEN

CALMING

In the last chapter, we talked about the two ways to approach healing. Remember, we can either choose to intentionally face our places of pain while in a peaceful state, or respond to a triggered moment and allow it to lead to healing. Both yield an opportunity for God to bring liberty to our souls. In the next three chapters, we are going to walk you through some very practical ways to partner with God's healing. These tools are available for you whether you are walking someone else through healing or you are pursuing healing for yourself. The goal is to partner with the Holy Spirit. He is the Comforter. He is the solution, and here are three ways the Holy Spirit can lead us to healing.

The first two steps are where you will want to start if you are in a triggered moment or are ministering to someone in a triggered state. Step three is where you begin if you are choosing to enter into trauma healing while in a place of peace.

Let's look at these steps one at a time.

STEP 1 - Comfort through Calming.

If you are in a triggered state, or you are ministering to someone in a triggered state, the first goal is to bring calm. Triggers are very unsettling, and calming must happen before anything else will be helpful. If someone is not breathing well, we don't try to reason with them; we need to help them come out of the trigger by calming them. It is usually the person's heart rate that needs to come down to a calm, regulated rhythm. Panic, anxiety, and triggers make our heart rate increase. Let's remember what a triggered state feels like. Emotions are heightened. Heart rate is escalating. Panic is threatening to set in, and it can feel very difficult to breathe. A triggered state can even feel like a heart attack.

Encourage yourself, or the person who is being triggered, to choose not to panic. A lot of times, a trigger begins to escalate because we become frightened about what we are feeling. Fear sets in about the things our body is experiencing, and that fear can make our bodies escalate into panic. If we predetermine to be as peaceful and kind to ourselves as possible, it helps keep the trigger from escalating unnecessarily.

Again, the logical first step is to bring calm. How do we do that? Well, one of the number one ways you can do that is through rhythm. Rhythm is very regulating. In utero, you heard the sound of your mom's heartbeat. The womb was a place of safety, peace, and calm. Our worldview was beginning to be formed from this place. Rhythm was a component of peace.

Think about how we pat babies on the back to help soothe them. You don't bring a baby to a place of calm by walking to their crib while they are crying and leaning over to yell, "Calm down, baby! I'm working on your bottle! I'll be right back! Take care of yourself for a minute!" Think about how you would soothe a baby. You would pick the baby up, hold him close to you, and pat his back. You might whisper to him, "Shhh, shhh, shhh." You might rock him, but you would never tell the baby to calm down and get over himself; it would not be very effective, nor kind.

But somehow we do this to people. We tell them to just calm down or get over it, or we quote Scripture at them when they are in a heightened, emotionally triggered state. It's so sad! Really, in those moments, we are communicating, "I don't have time for you. You are an inconvenience." We can also do this to ourselves with our own inner dialogue. We want you to think compassionate thoughts towards yourself and others.

Picture a baby that needs to be calmed. You would not look at a baby and think, "You little idiot, you got yourself into this mess in the first place." That sounds offensive, but so often that is the dialogue that happens in our hearts toward ourselves or others. When we look at babies, we see innocence. Innocence pulls on our compassion. We want you to know that is how Jesus looks at you, at all of us. We are His babies, and He sees our innocence, even though He already knows what is wrong and what happened to us. So be patient with yourself, and be patient with others.

Bring calm as gently as you would with a baby. There is a rhythm of patting that you can even do for yourself. Just patting your heart in a steady rhythm will help bring calm. Go ahead, try it just for a minute. Try patting yourself gently on your chest the way you would an innocent baby. Be patient and calm. Be kind and loving to yourself. Practice this for a moment; no one is looking. Just try it, and see if you feel any shift in your level of peace.

Do you see the effectiveness? You just created a memory of rhythm's helpfulness that will now be available to your mind if you ever find yourself in a triggered state. When it is challenging to think clearly, you have this memory to pull from.

Walking is another rhythm that can bring calm. If you start to feel a trigger coming on, you can try to keep it from escalating by going for a walk. Try to choose a casual stroll instead of an aerobic walk, with the intention of slowing your heart rate down.

Music also has rhythm that can bring calm. Now we obviously wouldn't recommend loud, aggressive music. Also, check with the triggered person to make sure they welcome music to help bring calm. Sometimes music is too much stimulation, so learn what is helpful to yourself or the other person. Anything that has a rhythm to it has the potential to bring calm and balance to a racing heartbeat.

Another very significant way to bring calm is by breathing. Breathing regulates our bodies. It is important to breathe slowly. Often, in a panicked state, you are not exhaling fully. You tend to hold your breath; therefore, breathing out slowly can calm your heart rate. It brings regulation and calm to just focus on your breathing. Thinking about your breathing gives your mind something to focus on. Breathing in, briefly holding your breath, and then breathing out slowly, can really calm your heartbeat down and bring regulation.

While we are talking about breathing, can we take a trip back to the Garden of Eden just for a moment? We want to really drive this home so you can understand just how powerful breathing is. We could be tempted to skip this step, but think about it, if we didn't have breath, what would happen? We would die! Breathing is very important. Who breathed the first breath? God. God is giving us a prescription, and He is also telling us who is the Giver of life.

"And the Lord God formed man of the dust of the ground and breathed into his nostrils the breath of life, and man became a living being" (Genesis 2:7).

Anything the Enemy brings is death, right? If God is inhalation, the Enemy is what? Exhalation. So, as we are breathing, we want to posture our hearts to think, "I am breathing in the life of God. As I am slowly breathing in the life of God, I am breathing everything out that stands in His way." See, it is different when you are putting your faith into action. Everything that God does breathes life into me, and everything that comes out of me doesn't belong. God is the Creator, and the Enemy is the abominator. God breathes life, and the Enemy wants to suck the life out. God goes in through the nose, and the Enemy goes out through the mouth. Faith, attached to such a simple action as breathing, can bring healing if we allow it.

Another calming element is touch. Touch can be really powerful in a heightened emotional state, but this is mostly true when you really know the person. This is an area that you want to tread carefully in a ministry setting, especially if you don't know the person very well. If the person is being triggered by something that has to do with being touched inappropriately, and your first instinct is to offer touch, it could cause the trigger to worsen. If you are ministering to someone you know, and it is a safe place, touch can be a very powerful tool.

Wiping tears, holding the person's hand, offering an embrace, or even just physical closeness (when appropriate), are all ways that touch can offer a great deal of calm. Think of how babies can be soothed through touch. Pick up a crying baby out of a crib, and they may already begin to calm down because help has arrived. Touch is grounding. In a triggered state, your brain doesn't always know when and where it is, but touch brings the person into the right now. It can be very helpful.

Gentle eye contact and a hug are two of the most effective ways to help someone calm. Think of a child needing to be soothed and calmed. We would pick that precious baby up, look at their sweet face, and help them know that they are safe, and it is going to be okay.

Be aware that in the calming stage, you are engaging with the lower part of the brain, and these lower parts of the brain may have been formed as a child. When this place gets triggered, the person may still respond as a child might because that is where the trauma was formed. Since you are engaging with someone in the part of their memory that was created when they were a child, there shouldn't be any condemnation over the person's behavior or needs.

You have to be able to step outside of the immediacy of the moment, outside of the comfort of your flesh, and step into what the Holy Spirit is doing so that you can help someone heal. It might make you feel vulnerable, but this is where we get over ourselves for the sake of another. We (Amber and Rachel) are both grown adult women, but we can't tell you how many times we have sat on the ground, in the grass, or on the floor of a church building while holding another grown adult in our arms as they weep in the fetal position. Not only should there be no judgment towards the other person or yourself, but we also have to know we are walking on very holy ground.

This is also true if **you** are the person who is healing. Allow yourself to yield to the leading of the Holy Spirit. If He asks you to pat your chest in order to bring yourself to a place of calm because He is trying to heal you, then pat your chest. If He wants you to allow someone to hug you or hold you while you cry, let Him lead that too. If He asks you to lay down the internal script of what you think should happen, and follow Him into the unknown; do it. When we humble ourselves and yield to God as our Great Physician, He will use these moments to do miraculous things on our behalf.

He will heal and redeem and rescue. Oh, the stories of His glory we have seen in these moments! Don't miss them because you're afraid to yield to Him. Just yield. Just breathe.

CHAPTER ELEVEN

CONNECTING

Once you have engaged with the calming methods, and you can see that they are beginning to help bring regulation and a steady heart rate, you can proceed with the next step.

STEP 2 - Comfort through Connecting

The next step in bringing comfort is **connecting**. The heart behind this step is to help a triggered person connect with the present moment. We do this by bringing awareness to their present surroundings and helping them connect with the Holy Spirit and with the person walking them through this process.

To begin connecting, speak with soothing, slow tones. Remember that we are potentially engaging with a person who is currently experiencing a child's mindset and emotional response. Be sure not to riddle them with information. Don't speak harshly or loudly, and avoid anything abrasive or jolting. Communicate with peace and intentionality.

We also want to speak with direction. Our words need to lead the person somewhere. We need to offer them a pathway. What we say to them should gently guide them to come back to a place of calm. As we are connecting, we must also choose to walk in our spirit by listening to the guidance of the Holy Spirit as we communicate in peace.

Let's say that you and a friend are hanging out together at a grocery store. Out of the blue, your friend starts to have a panic attack. You have a choice to make. You can join them in the panic, or you can walk in your spirit. It is a choice to be able to say, "Okay, I am going to walk in the fruit of the Spirit of peace because my friend needs me." It can be very jolting to you, as a friend, to watch someone you love become suddenly triggered. If you aren't walking with the Spirit of God, in your own spirit, you won't have the capacity to be helpful. Choosing to be aware of the Holy Spirit and connecting with His peace will help you to stay calm.

Having a panic attack or a trauma trigger feels scary. Have you ever experienced one of these episodes? You were doing great, then suddenly, you couldn't catch your breath, and it felt as if you were having a heart attack or possibly dying. It is very scary, and any person might face a great deal of fear in that moment. These attacks may also cause a person to feel like they are going insane. Thoughts may spiral as the person questions, "Am I going crazy? Out of the blue, my body is just freaking out. One minute ago, I was completely fine, and now I don't know what is happening, but I feel crazy!" Why does a trigger cause this type of reaction? It's because that is what a trigger is, it is a "suddenly." It just comes in like a gunshot and starts the cycle of a heightened arousal state inside a person's body, and it feels absolutely out of control.

As the helper in this situation, we stay at peace, and then we focus on eye contact. Make sure you are using gentle eye contact, as if you are looking into the eyes of an infant. Remember, the trauma that is being triggered may have happened in their little hood, in their childhood. You may be looking directly into the eyes of a person who is back in a childhood state, where the trauma first formed. In this very critical moment, you have the opportunity to help them through your response, with the direction and tone of your words, and with the way you choose to make eye contact with them while you are walking in your spirit.

You can actually help to change their worldview in this triggered moment. Just by the way you're looking at them, you can change their worldview. Imagine that. By your words, tone, eye contact, proximity, and presence, you can help reshape their worldview and bring healing to the part of their heart that was so deeply wounded. Have you ever heard one of your loved ones tell a personal story of intense pain and longed to have the power to change that for them and take the pain away? In these unexpected yet critical moments, when they are experiencing a trigger, you have the opportunity to help that pain lift from their life. Talk about miraculous!

I (Rachel) adopted all of my children. I often listen to them tell stories of things they experienced before they were mine, and it breaks my heart. I so desperately long to have been there with them and to have had the opportunity to create a different experience for their little hearts. God has often comforted me, as their mom, with the understanding that being present with them as they process through their painful memories is actually healing what was and rewriting it with what is now. I have connected with them while they were in a triggered state and had the divine opportunity to speak right to those childhood memories with comfort, peace, love, and calm. The Comforter is so present in those moments, and I am deeply thankful for the opportunity of redemption for my children.

The next key to bringing comfort through connecting is to bring the person's awareness into the right now. Bring them into the present moment because "when" they are, during an active trigger, is not in the present moment. You want to help ground that person in the truth of where they currently are. You can do this by telling them, "You are here. You are right here." Do anything that comes to your mind that will help bring their senses into the awareness of right now.

One way you can do this is with a gentle touch. Very softly, being careful not to be jolting, soothingly place your hand on their arm or their hand. Do this slowly, with your eyes focused on them, so that they know you're coming in closer. Again, keep your gentle eyes on them, and tell them, "It's all right. It's going to be okay. I'm here. You're right here with me." Gentle touch causes their senses to activate and adds new information into the brain processes. The presence of new information in the brain helps rinse out what caused the trigger.

In bringing comfort through connecting, we want to assure the person that they are safe, and no one is going to hurt them. Help them to understand that this moment will pass. It will not last forever. You can validate that what they are feeling is real, but it will pass. You can say, "What you are feeling is real, but it is not based on today's truth or reality, and it will pass. It is going to be okay."

Bring assurance that they are not alone. A lot of trauma happens in a place of isolation. No one else was there but you, your pain, and whoever caused it. It can feel helpless and hopeless. Part of what makes traumatic events so painful is the isolation and feeling of being alone. There is not only the loneliness of experiencing the trauma but also of living with it and trying to manage it alone for so long. God wants that to shift. The pain of isolation and loneliness is tormenting, and a significant part of healing is simply not being alone in the pain.

It is so important that we help, even help ourselves as the helpers, send the message that we are not alone. If no human is there with you, you are still not alone. The Comforter is always there with you. We want to assure the person, "Never again will you face that moment and be alone." We want to help them believe that the Comforter is there with them, and we are there with them. Using the same gentle tones, you can say things like, "You are not alone. I am here. Jesus is here. His Spirit is here with us."

It is very helpful to bring attention to the fact that the Holy Spirit is with us because every encounter with Him provides an opportunity for healing and change. If you experience something in isolation, but later encounter the memory of it with the presence of God as your companion, it creates a new memory. This new memory experience becomes a new point of reference and causes the neurons in our brain to begin reorganizing. The wiring in our brains actually starts to shift. Strongholds built in the pain of isolation begin to crumble when we encounter the Comforter. Memories that started out laced with fear and torment now have the added information and experience of the Holy Spirit, His love, and His comfort.

God wants to dispel our fears. He wants us to realize we have nothing to be afraid of. We want to help encourage you even with how you process the word "trigger." Can we help you change your mind about the word "trigger," and let it be associated with the idea of opportunity rather than torment?

Every triggered moment, every moment of heightened arousal state, when your nervous system is engaged, is an opportunity for healing. Each time you press into that moment for healing, and follow that breadcrumb trail, you'll see things differently. You won't experience that same moment in that same way ever again. It is going to change because now you are walking through those moments hand in hand with God. Gradually, the triggers will dissipate, your emotions will no longer respond to those memories, and you will have holy closure.

What you are doing is helping to build resiliency. You're helping to reshape the person's worldview. Remember, our words need to have intentionality; they are meant to take the person somewhere. Think of the sentence, "You're not alone." Do these words take the person somewhere? Yes, they take them into the right now, reminding them that they are with someone new, whether that is the Holy Spirit or someone else as well. What about, "You're safe." This is clear direction because it reminds them that where they were when something really bad happened to them felt unsafe, but right now, they **are** safe. You can repeat it as many times as you need to. "Right now, right here, you are safe." We are guiding them with Holy Spirit-led words to help the brain process in a healthy way, enabling them to move past the triggered part of their brain and into the prefrontal cortex, which brings awareness of their present reality.

One of the most important things we can tell you is to be patient. Healing can be a process. The person you are walking with throughout this process deserves patience, and you deserve to give yourself patience as you work towards your own healing with the Holy Spirit. Any person who needs our help deserves patience, so don't be in a hurry. If you feel rushed you must stop and assess your own heart for a moment. If there is anything in you that thinks, "Man, this person should be getting this already," ask yourself where that thought comes from. Impatience is a red flag that shows you are not walking in your spirit.

We have to stay in a place of peace, knowing that there is a person with a wounded heart in front of us. If they feel our impatience, what does that teach them about trying to heal? We are helping them create a worldview of what healing looks like. They may never try again if we aren't careful and patient. If we respond incorrectly, we can wound and traumatize that person further instead of ushering them toward healing.

Healing is like stepping out of the dark cave of self-protection, one inch at a time, until we are completely vulnerable before the light and love of the Lord. That takes a great deal of trust. When you walk in your spirit, that person can sense it. Once that person trusts you, a beautiful waltz in the spirit begins to happen, and healing is the priceless result. But if you break that bond in the spirit and get in your flesh, that person can feel it, which can be very wounding. So be extremely patient with yourself and others.

Connecting is a really important step, and it shouldn't be rushed. Calming and connecting help to arrest the escalation of a trigger. Don't forget that in these moments of connecting during a trigger, your involvement can help reshape the person's worldview. Where they knew trauma and pain, they can now experience love, gentleness, kindness, and peace. You become an ambassador of love for that person. You can help to create a new standard of what love and care look like.

Your embrace and loving eyes may be the first expression of pure love a person has ever experienced. Never underestimate the potency of a simple embrace. You may be engaging with a part of a person's mind and soul that has never experienced love. In these moments, trauma is healing. It is actually healing. The part of the soul that was previously trapped in trauma is gaining a new understanding and replacing a painful experience with a peaceful one. In these moments, Jesus is actively exchanging ashes for beauty.

CHAPTER TWELVE

COMMUNICATING

We have already covered two of the important pathways that lead to healing from trauma. The first option was to enter into healing while you are in a place of peace, during a non-triggered moment. You may prefer to journey into the memories associated with trauma with just you and the Holy Spirit, or you may choose a safe person to bring alongside you on this journey.

The second option was to allow a triggered moment to become an opportunity for healing. We walked through how to go from a triggered place, to a calm place, and then to a connected place.

Whether we started from a triggered moment or from a place of simply choosing, communication is the intersection of those pathways to healing. Communication is where you start with someone who is not in a triggered state and with someone who has walked through a trigger into a calm and connected place.

Step 3 - Comfort through Communicating

Communication begins when the person experiencing a trigger has become more regulated and isn't in the height of an arousal or shut down state. It is important not to rush to the communication step because you can't offer wisdom or counsel to someone who isn't in a calm and connected state. No matter how brilliant you are, no matter how much wonderful insight you have, the person doesn't have the capacity to communicate with you until they are in a more regulated state of mind.

The shift into communicating often launches when the triggered person begins to share what is happening. Encourage the person to share what triggered them or where they feel like they may have trauma present. For example, what emotion are they feeling? Is there a memory, image, or word attached to what they were feeling? Any of these pieces of information are guidance as to where the Holy Spirit might be moving in the person's life. Give them plenty of space to share; it might take them time to find their words and fully express what was happening. Maintain your gentle eye contact, and listen intently, giving them your full attention. This part cannot be rushed and requires patience.

As they are communicating, you are listening for several things. Most importantly, you are listening to what the Holy Spirit is saying to you and through them. You are listening for breadcrumbs that might lead you to the root of what is happening. Pray quietly in your spirit, asking the Holy Spirit to give you the insight, revelation, and understanding that is needed to help the person gain freedom. You are also listening for lies of the Enemy that might be present, strongholds in the person's thinking, and for the presence of any demonic influence. You must be listening through your spirit to discern correctly. When it is the Holy Spirit, the understanding will come through a lens of compassion, not judgment. Let that be your guide to know when thoughts are from Him versus your own reasoning or personal knowledge of the person's history.

For instance, one person we were ministering to was triggered by hearing a few lyrics of a song. She only remembered a few words and couldn't immediately identify the song. She just felt such sadness and couldn't understand why she was crying and feeling so panicked. After she was able to come down into a place of calm and was connected, she did a search of those few lyrics, and it led her to a Kermit the Frog video on YouTube. As she watched the video of the song, an entire trauma memory opened up to her understanding. As she talked through the details of her trauma, she shared about the deep hopelessness she had felt during her abusive childhood. As we ministered to that place of trauma, we were also able to identify demonic strongholds and influences. This journey into healing and deliverance all started with a song…sung by a frog.

Sometimes the shift into communicating happens through the discernment of the Holy Spirit. We want to give the Holy Spirit room to move. You have to know the difference between the Holy Spirit offering you insight that He intends for you to ponder in your own heart and when He gives you information He plans for you to speak out loud, into the situation. The Holy Spirit is very clear, and you will feel Him moving and hear Him speaking. If you are drawing a blank, that means you don't need to say a thing. Don't be intimidated by silence. Sometimes the silence is the Holy Spirit letting you know He doesn't need your assistance because He is speaking directly to the person Himself.

There are many vehicles that the Holy Spirit might want to use to communicate to you. Don't ignore the pressure in your chest, an image you might see, or even lyrics to a song. When an impression doesn't seem to go away, the Holy Spirit may be trying to get your attention. You can trust Him and follow His lead.

Holy Spirit may give you words and tell you to say something like this, "You are worthy of love, worthy of love." Once you offer those words, pause and test whether or not the words hit a target by watching the person's response. Remember, human reasoning is not what we are after, so navigating carefully with the Holy Spirit is of the utmost importance. Even if it seems clear what the trigger was or what wisdom may be needed, let's always follow the leading of the Holy Spirit. When He is leading, there will be grace on a person's ears to hear, even if they are still coming out of a triggered state. The effectiveness is not found in the individual; it is found in trusting the profound accuracy of the Holy Spirit.

Once communication has begun, there are several helpful elements to include. First, we want to impart truth and wisdom. It is not that we come at the person with condemning truth or phrases full of "shoulds," that sound like, "You should this... or you should that." It usually sounds more like, "You are worthy of love. Jesus is with you. He is here for you. He wants to heal you. He has freedom for you." We are to offer truth and wisdom. We are listening for Jesus to speak to us. We are following the breadcrumbs to get to the root of what the trigger was. We are not necessarily asking for dialogue; we are speaking truth over them and strengthening them. We are affirming their identity in Christ and offering comfort while asking the Holy Spirit for the truth and wisdom needed to combat the lie or stronghold that may be present.

Let's pause here and get some understanding on what we mean when we use the word *stronghold*. A stronghold is a narrative or a fortress where our beliefs live. A stronghold guides the way we think and live.

"The Lord is my light and my salvation: whom shall I fear? The Lord is the stronghold of my life; of whom shall I be afraid?" (Psalms 27:1).

What do we call the Enemy's attack against our mind? It is a stronghold, yet we read in the Scripture above that the **Lord** is the stronghold of my life. Imagine that the Enemy constructs a stronghold around your trauma because he doesn't want you to gain freedom. He wants it to feel like a prison, and he doesn't want the truth to get in. The Enemy's stronghold may be a prison, but when the Word of God begins to enter in, it breaks down that stronghold one piece at a time. Afterwards, God's truth becomes the stronghold of your life. It becomes the protector so that the Enemy can't get in. God is a shield. He is working on your behalf to keep the Enemy from coming back into that place. We have to commit in our hearts to allow the Word of God to be our stronghold. His truth protects us from every lie of the Enemy.

The Holy Spirit will also alert us to every untruth we are believing. He is light, and He will shine his light on our behalf and say, "See this thing you're believing? It is not true. You are worthy of love. It doesn't matter what has happened to you; I still say you are worthy. I would die a suffering death on the Cross, even if it were just for you. That is how worthy of love you are." You have to understand that He is light. Trauma is like a dark cave, and He is like the flashlight telling you, "Come this way. You are worthy of love.

You are safe. You are not alone." As you follow His light, you will come out of the darkness and into the full impact of His truth.

"Your word is a lamp to my feet, And a light to my path" (Psalm 119:105).

Speaking truth is not necessarily about having a conversation that requires reasoning with the person. In faith, you are to speak truth into the soul of the person so that it might combat the lies that have become a fortress for the Enemy. You are not giving a lecture or a full discourse on the whole topic that they might be working to overcome. What is the Holy Spirit saying at this specific moment? It doesn't take a plethora of words to accomplish this part. Simplicity will suffice in this context. Imparting truth is partnering with God to stimulate the neuroplasticity of the person's brain. God's truth is what is essential and fundamental to healing.

"And you shall know the truth, and the truth shall set you free." (John 8:32).

We might also identify areas where the Enemy has stolen vocabulary. The Enemy wants to stake a claim on anything he can, and he wants to possess vocabulary. Take the word *love*, for instance. He wants to abominate the word *love* and turn it into something completely different. One simple word can be the beginning of an unholy narrative. The Enemy wants to create a running dialogue of deception in your mind by claiming one word at a time and giving each one a distorted definition. This is his scheme, to build strongholds in our minds with one brick, or one word, at a time. Everything God creates, the Enemy wants to abominate. He is not a creator. He is an abominator. The Enemy wants to come in and overshadow everything that God says by covering it up with his lies. He wants to distract you from the truth because that is who he is. He is the Father of Lies, and you allow the Enemy to become your foster parent when you believe any word that he says. The Enemy is seated upon a throne in any area of our thoughts where we have failed to challenge him. With every word he claims, his evil throne increases in size. He absolutely needs to be dethroned from each area of our life where he has been allowed to sit in a place of authority over God's truth.

2 Corinthians 10:5 (NIV) says, *"We demolish arguments and every pretension that sets itself up against the knowledge of God, and we take captive every thought to make it obedient to Christ."*

"Who's your daddy?" "Who is the father of this thought?" These are questions we can ask ourselves and others. If a thought doesn't stem from the truth, it doesn't stay. Is the thought from the Father of Unconditional Love or the Father of Lies? Where did it come from? Where are you gaining this education? If it doesn't pass the test of love and truth, it has to go.

With that in mind, when we are walking with someone through trauma, we are also listening for vocabulary that the Enemy may have stolen. Here is a great example through the word *obey*. A friend of ours was driving in the car and saw the word *obey* on a billboard, and it triggered something in her. This person was abused by a step-parent who distorted the Word of God by telling his children that, according to scripture, God wanted them to comply in obedience while he was abusing them. We can clearly see that the word *obey* is on the table. Can you discern, based on the word *obey*, what truth needs to be imparted to counteract this lie?

Pop quiz! We really want you to pause and ask the Holy Spirit to show you what truth you would offer to this person. Really give yourself an opportunity, and don't move on until you have an answer.

Ready for some insight?

"Children, if you want to be wise, listen to your parents and do what they tell you, and the Lord will help you. For the commandment, 'Honor your father and your mother,' was the first of the Ten Commandments with a promise attached: 'You will prosper and live a long, full life if you honor your parents'" (Ephesians 6:1-3 TPT).

But wait… there's more…

Verse 4 says, *"Fathers, don't exasperate your children, but raise them up with loving discipline and counsel that brings the revelation of our Lord."*

The Word of God has promises attached to the word *obey*. Furthermore, it has instructions to the fathers that immediately follow. Seeing His Word in context helped the person understand that God's heart for obedience also includes His instructions to not harm children. Reclaiming the vocabulary helped the person process the memory in a healthy way. Trauma lifted off, and the word *obey* reclaimed its rightful place as a word full of promise.

The next part of communicating is commanding any trauma trapped in the person's body to lift off. Walk in your authority as one who is seated with Christ in heavenly places (Ephesians 2:6). Keep speaking in peaceful tones because volume does not equate to authority. You can simply say, "Trauma lift." Feel permission to call it all out. You don't know how deeply ingrained trauma may be within the person's body. Ask the Holy Spirit to agitate any place of trauma until it lifts completely off of the person. In Christ, feel free to say, "Lift from this body. Lift from this brain. Lift from this soul. Lift from these cells. Lift from the blood. Lift from the marrow." That really is it. If you are walking in your authority and being led by the Spirit, it doesn't take fancy, perfect prayers. Simple commands are perfect. "Trauma lift."

Don't be alarmed if the person is responding in a heightened way. Shaking, deep crying, travailing, and sometimes screaming can be normal responses. Trauma may create a really deep, painful sound when it lifts off. These responses are common. Don't be concerned, wondering how to react in the midst of what's happening. Let's go over the obvious ways that you can respond. First, stay in your spirit. Don't check out. This isn't the time to run to the bathroom. Next, stay present with the person. Don't let yourself get disconcerted; Finally, keep being gentle and kind, and consistently offer soothing eye contact.

What can you say? What can you offer them when they are in this state? You can offer comforting words like, "You're all right. I'm here. You're going to be fine." You're basically there as a midwife. Think of yourself as a nursemaid, assisting the Holy Spirit as He births something new and healthy within the person. It can be a little startling to witness decades of pain and trauma coming off of a person, so it is important to be aware that this is what deliverance can look and sound like.

Now what? Now what do you think should happen? Do you think this ministry event has come to its end?

Not quite yet. After we tell trauma to lift, we shift into the next part. We have talked about how the devil is a punk and a bully. He doesn't care that you have had trauma. He is coming in with his demons to reinforce your pain and keep you in pain for as long as you have breath in your body. We have to know that with trauma, there is likely always a demonic spirit attached to it. The process isn't over when trauma lifts. We have to pop the whole disgusting zit. All of it has to come out. The trauma attached to the physical body is tormenting, but so are the demonic spirits that reinforce the trauma. If we don't tell the demonic to lift, the person may go home and feel the same way. We have to command any unholy spirit to come out as well.

You may get specific insight into the spirit that is hiding behind the lies, strongholds, or situations that caused trauma. What spirit is associated with the specific trauma you are dealing with? Let's use the example of the word *obey*. The word *obey* was a vocabulary word that triggered trauma. What demonic spirit would be behind trauma attached to that word? Well, the Holy Spirit brought us understanding, and a religious spirit and all of the demonic kingdom attached to it, a spirit of abuse, a spirit of incest, a spirit of fear, a spirit of intimidation, and a spirit of torment came off of this specific person.

We couldn't give you a list of every kind of spirit that will "always" be associated with trauma, but we can tell you that torment is almost always present where there has been trauma. Neither one of us (Amber or Rachel) can recall a time when we have ministered to a person who was being healed and delivered from trauma, where a spirit of torment was not also evicted. We aren't saying it is a law or that you will never encounter something different, but it is helpful to know that when you are ministering to someone who has lived under the effects of trauma, you need to check for a spirit of torment, and command it to lift off of the person.

Here is an example of how you could pray for deliverance with someone during this step of trauma healing. "I command you to lift now; you may no longer continue to function in this person. All evidence of your existence, every place you have touched, is being wiped and cleansed by the Holy Spirit right now. Every organ, every tissue, every brain synapse be cleansed now in Jesus' name." We want all the fingerprints of the demonic to be removed from that person's life.

This is a very opportune time to walk in our authority as believers. We have the ability to establish how the Enemy should leave. He doesn't get to choose how he leaves. We are not going to allow the person to go through unnecessary thrashing about. We are going to command all demonic spirits to leave through the breath so that the person is not further traumatized by the dramatic antics of the Enemy. God is the giver of life. His breath is life. He breathed life into the nostrils of Adam. The Enemy can't create. He isn't life; he is death. He is exhalation. We command the Enemy to come out through the breath. We declare that he doesn't have permission to cause harm to the person upon his exit.

During this process, we are going to maintain a comforting and peaceful tone and calming body language. Avoid loud, abrupt, or sudden movements such as clapping, snapping, pointing, or pacing. The last thing you want to do is yell at a demon while commanding it to leave, when a person is healing from verbal abuse. We don't need to use theatrics to draw attention to ourselves. We can take someone through healing and deliverance in a very calm, patient way.

The next thing we want to do is impart comfort. Trauma has lifted. Demons have lifted. Now we want to impart comfort, so we speak comfort and love over the person and ask the Holy Spirit to fill those places that were just ministered to. We ask Him to provide everything that was lacking because of this trauma and everything this person needed in the past but didn't receive. And we ask that everything the Enemy stole be returned back to them.

"But if he's caught, he still has to pay back what he stole sevenfold; his punishment and fine will cost him greatly" (Proverbs 6:31 TPT).

We ask the Holy Spirit to impart His comfort, to hold them, and to fill them with His love. We ask the Holy Spirit to freshly baptize the person with His love. We speak rest and peace to those pieces. Rest and peace to the places of trauma. We ask God to create new paths in their mind as He heals their physical brain. We ask Him to create new neural pathways where this trauma was originally located and to close this door with finality as He brings healing to that part of the mind. We can have faith that they don't have to experience a trigger with that specific memory in that way ever again.

What a miracle to have walked through trauma into this place. Would you believe the best part is still to come? That's right, our favorite part is in the next chapter. Wait until you see what it is.

CHAPTER THIRTEEN

RESCUE

This may be our favorite chapter. Well, it is probably a toss-up between this one and the chapter about the Comforter. This chapter is special because it is about the One our hearts adore; it's about our King. It's about our Jesus and how He works these beautiful miracles of love in the hearts of His precious lambs.

Oh, Beloved, can you feel the anticipation?

So much understanding, process, and healing has been covered in the previous pages. But this chapter needs its own breathing space. The final step, dare we say the most important piece in this process, is connecting a person's heart to their rescuer, who is Jesus.

After having calmed, connected, and communicated with the comfort of the Holy Spirit, keep the person engaged just a little longer. If you are the one who is processing, linger still. You will not want to miss out on what is about to happen.

We are going to ask Jesus to redeem the memory of the trauma He just walked you through. How do we do this? Start by asking the person to close their eyes and connect with the memory they were just experiencing. Even if it started with a word, image, or sound, ask them to invite the Holy Spirit to unveil what memory this evocative cue was connected to. Now that the torment and trauma have lifted, we want to take advantage of this opportunity for them to experience fullness and healing in this part of their heart.

As the person connects with the memory, find out what they are seeing and feeling? Have them press as far into that memory as they can. Now ask them to look for Jesus. Where was Jesus? What was Jesus doing, and where was He in the midst of the traumatic memory? You can be sure that Jesus has something to say, and we are creating the space for Him to express His words and offer His insight into their circumstance.

Pray a simple prayer of agreement. "Jesus, we join our faith right now with Yours and ask You to reveal Yourself, reveal Your heart, reveal Your words for this person, and reveal Your presence in this memory because we know You are there."

The person may be praying this prayer through tears. Everything may still feel fresh, or the person might be experiencing a bit of shock, thinking, "I didn't even remember this until it got triggered!" That happens, so don't be alarmed. You can get triggered into a memory that you didn't even have a conscious awareness of and find yourself in the midst of all the emotions and physical responses connected to it. It can be shocking.

Also factor in the knowledge that through the power of the Holy Spirit, a demon just left your body, and trauma released its hold on you. This can all feel stunning and disorienting, especially if you didn't even know trauma was present or that you could experience deliverance at all. Regardless of the shock and disoriented feeling, this moment is ripe with the opportunity for healing, and this is the primary healing we want to lead the person into.

We need to be gentle and loving, and lead them to connect with Jesus. Keep asking God questions like, "Jesus, where were you in the room during this memory? Show me where you were in this place. You are omnipresent; show me where you were in this moment. Show me how you would have responded. Tell me what you would have said. Show me what you would have done."

Give space for this to happen. Don't rush it. This is very holy.

Do you remember everything we have learned about the brain so far? Connecting Jesus into the memory of the traumatic moment is so important to the rewiring of the brain. What is happening is that the Enemy is being extracted, and now a new memory is created. Now, when that memory is recalled at a later date, the memory includes Jesus and what He did to rescue the person out of the situation. Connecting Jesus and His comforting presence to the memory creates a new memory for the person and a new connection to that event and those evocative cues. This is especially true during a triggered moment because that specific part of the brain and memory bank are being activated.

Inside the memory, Jesus will often make Himself known to the person. He will walk into the room, pick them up out of their pain, hold them, or speak words of tender love to them. Sometimes he destroys whatever was causing pain. He brings truth into the room and into their hearts. In one specific person's experience, she recalls Jesus taking her by the hand and walking her out of each room where a painful memory had happened. He also gave her a visual understanding that buckets of His precious blood would be used to wash away the memory of the pain. After this holy moment, a new precedent is set. Jesus' presence trumps the pain, and in place of the prison, His rescue becomes the focus. His presence washes and cleanses the memories. His cleansing flood brings peace and rest for the soul.

"When the enemy comes in like a flood, The Spirit of the Lord will lift up a standard against him" (Isaiah 59:19)

Jesus lives outside of time; so you can believe that what He shows you is really where He was. It is not a fantasy. Again, this is really where He was. He has the capacity to take you on a journey back to that moment, revisit it with you, and lay a new memory in your mind. He can show you the reality of where He was and what He was doing. Even if you can't recall the visual memory from that moment, from here forward, you will. Now it will include where Jesus was and how He was rescuing you. This is the ultimate healing. Now when the memory surfaces, it will include the presence of the

Lord. What a gift! He erases the torment and replaces it with His presence, and He is the Prince of Peace.

"And His name will be called Wonderful Counselor, Mighty God, Eternal Father, Prince of Peace" (Isaiah 9:6b).

Every one of these moments allows the person's heart to bond with God. Isn't it incredible what God can do with something the Enemy meant to harm you? (Genesis 50:20) No matter how many shards of glass, broken places, or wounded pieces, Jesus can take what the Enemy meant as torment and turn it into a place where you have now bonded to His love and His heart.

We are meant to bond with God in our healing. Remember all of those feel-good bonding chemicals in our brains? It is not just about having the pain removed; it is about receiving His love in its place and all the pleasure that comes with that promise. Healing is more than having a deficit and coming back to baseline. There was a deep wound, and the Lord redeemed it. You are now able to say, "He brought me recompense by coming into this place with me, healing it, and establishing Himself there. He took me so far past a baseline of normalcy that I now have bonded with my Creator in this moment. I have encountered Heaven."

What is happening as God reveals himself in memories is real because He lives outside of time. When God, Himself, walks into my memory and establishes Himself as my stronghold, that is healing. We bond with God through the process when we discover that He is the one who rescues. His face becomes imprinted on our hearts. His hands reach into the darkness to lift us out, and His Spirit, love, comfort, and presence impress themselves upon us in those moments. Healing bonds us to our King, and we get to know Him as our rescuer.

We can tell you the story of a person who experienced severe sexual abuse. The Lord worked His miraculous love and brought rescue to their memories associated with the trauma, exactly the way we are talking about here. Now when you ask the person what they remember about those moments, what they will describe to you is a completely different story. In those moments, they now see Jesus sitting cross-legged on their bed. They see His tears streaming down His cheeks. He is holding them, rocking them, and weeping over them while singing songs of redemption and love over pieces of their heart. He then stands up, carries them out of that room, and shuts the door. Remember the Scripture about Jesus being touched by our infirmities (Hebrews 4:15)? This person got to tangibly experience His compassion, and this Scripture became part of their personal history with their Savior, Redeemer, and now Rescuer. This precious little heart got to experience that firsthand. What a miracle!

Isn't that beautiful? You can ask Jesus to show you where He was even in memories you might not consider to be traumatic. If you have painful pieces in your past, your King wants to come into all of those places of pain, and show you where His love is healing and rescuing. Do you have painful memories that you would love to be made new as God floods your mind with love and comfort? Beloved, this is for you!

Did you know that Jesus even did this with the disciples? He is such a Shepherd. He knew that He was about to go to the Cross, and even as He prepared to lay down His life for all of mankind, He was wholeheartedly interested in loving and preparing His disciples for what they were about to experience. They were about to witness a brutal, torturous murder – HIS MURDER! But what did Jesus do in preparation? He created a memory with them as He washed their feet.

"Jesus knew that the night before Passover would be his last night on earth before leaving this world to return to the Father's side. All throughout his time with his disciples, Jesus had demonstrated a deep and tender love for them. And now he longed to show them the full measure of his love. Before their evening meal had begun, the accuser had already deeply embedded betrayal into the heart of Judas Iscariot, the son of Simon.

Jesus was fully aware that the Father had placed all things under his control, for he had come from God and was about to go back to be with him. So he got up from the meal and took off his outer robe, and took a towel and wrapped it around his waist. Then he poured water into a basin and began to wash the disciples' dirty feet and dry them with his towel.

But when Jesus got to Simon Peter, he objected and said, "I can't let you wash my dirty feet—you're my Lord!"

Jesus replied, "You don't understand yet the meaning of what I'm doing, but soon it will be clear to you."

107

Peter looked at Jesus and said, "You'll never wash my dirty feet—never!"

"But Peter, if you don't allow me to wash your feet," Jesus responded, "then you will not be able to share life with me."

So Peter said, "Lord, in that case, don't just wash my feet, wash my hands and my head too!"

Jesus said to him, "You are already clean. You've been washed completely and you just need your feet to be cleansed—but that can't be said of all of you." For Jesus knew which one was about to betray him, and that's why he told them that not all of them were clean.

After washing their feet, he put his robe on and returned to his place at the table. "Do you understand what I just did?" Jesus said. "You've called me your teacher and Lord, and you're right, for that's who I am. So if I'm your teacher and Lord and have just washed your dirty feet, then you should follow the example that I've set for you and wash one another's dirty feet. Now do for each other what I have just done for you. I speak to you timeless truth: a servant is not superior to his master, and an apostle is never greater than the one who sent him. So now put into practice what I have done for you, and you will experience a life of happiness enriched with untold blessings!" (John 13:1-17 TPT).

Jesus comforted His disciples in advance. He comforted them and instructed them to comfort each other. He was preparing them for what was coming. He was preparing them to serve and love each other in the midst of a trauma. He was creating a memory for them to connect back to that would show them where He was and what He would be doing if He were with them.

"Then he raised a cup and gave thanks to God and said to them, 'Take this and pass it on to one another and drink. I promise you that the next time we drink this wine, we will be together in the feast of God's kingdom.' Then he lifted up a loaf, and after praying a prayer of thanksgiving to God, he gave each of his apostles a piece of bread, saying, 'This loaf is my body, which is now being offered to you. Always eat it to remember me'" (Luke 22:17-19 TPT).

Here at the Last Supper, Jesus was also preparing His disciples to endure the pain that was about to come to them by giving them a visual memory to hold on to. When they were dismayed and in shock and disbelief about the traumatic grief they were enduring at the loss of their Rabbi, they had this memory to reflect on. They had this memory to help them know that Jesus knew what was going to happen and wasn't surprised by it. He wanted them to have a memory with Him that comforted their hearts.

Can you see, even as we are talking about the brain, that Jesus took all these things into account with His disciples? He made a memory with them that engaged their senses. From that moment on, every time they smelled bread, they thought of Him. Every time they sipped wine, they had that memory of Him. Remember Granny's spearmint gum, Bengay, and mothballs? Remember the comfort foods? Jesus created His own memory by laying out this supper for His disciples.

Jesus made sure to engage all of His disciples' senses to make certain they had a full, comfort-infused memory to fall back on. He gave them the smell of bread, flavor of wine, taste of both, feel of His hands washing their feet as He wiped off dust and debris, sound of the water as His hand stirred the bowl, and the visual of Jesus outing a mutiny formed against Him without being intimidated by it. He created a memory that told his disciples that no lie can stay hidden when He is in the room. As long as He is present, the lies will be exposed, and everything the Enemy meant for evil, He will turn it around for their good. He taught them to do this for others, to wash the trauma from His people, and cleanse them from the lies of the Enemy. We have equal rights to this memory because we are also His disciples.

Our memories matter to Him.

Think about all of the strategies and insight the Lord could have offered to His beloved disciples in the hours before He went to the Cross. He could have told them exactly what was coming during the rest of their days on earth, what they should do to avoid pain entirely, or how to most quickly advance the Kingdom. He didn't. He brought them to a place of peace. He connected with them and communicated with them. Our precious King and Savior looked them all in the eyes as He washed their feet and broke bread with them. He made memories with them so that they would have those images to bring them comfort.

He will do the same with our memories if we allow Him. He will lead us to them, show us where He was in the room and what He had to say about what was happening. He will rescue us and let us have that visual memory to go along with the rescue. He will bring comfort to us through our memories if we will allow Him. He is inviting us to taste and see that He is good (Psalm 34:8). Every time you remember, you are tasting and seeing that He is good. The new memory that He has created for you is your refuge, your safe place.

Will you allow Him? Will you let Him into those places? Can you imagine the beautiful tapestry of heaven-colored memories you could have if He was invited to participate in them with you?

The Enemy is not stronger than the Lord. We aren't just hoping Jesus can clean up the mess that the devil made. Jesus is not only going to destroy the works of the devil, He is going to give you restitution.

Don't stop before the restitution.
Don't stop before the restoration.
Don't stop before the recompense.

In those moments, God is giving you a piece of who you are in Heaven as you are seated with Him in heavenly places. You are encountering Heaven. You are encountering part of your destiny. *On Earth as it is in Heaven* is happening for you in that moment. Don't stop short of this part. Let the damage of the Enemy dissipate, and let the memory now be of the loving King Jesus, coming to rescue His little lamb.

"Manifest your kingdom realm, and cause your every purpose to be fulfilled on earth, just as it is in heaven" (Matthew 6:10 TPT).

Does this not feel miraculous? The redemption of God is an absolute miracle. Can you see it? We have cried out for revival. We have cried out to see the hand of God move. We long to witness miracles and watch heaven invade the darkness of this world as we move in His power. We want to see limbs grow back, autism lift, and hardened hearts turn to Jesus. The Bride of Christ aches to be reunited with her Groom. Our spirits cry out to function in the fullness they were created for. We know, we ache, and we long for far more than what we see around us.

Friend, do you see that this is a blueprint for how to walk someone into a miracle? It might not have as much pomp and circumstance as a stage in an arena with thousands of people who witness a person get up out of a wheelchair; though that is incredible, and we celebrate it. But to that one person you are ministering to… oh, what love they feel! What an opportunity! What a miracle! Can you see the opportunities for miracles that are in front of your face on a daily basis when we stop for the one in front of us and enter into their pain with them? Miracles of healing can happen in the dozens, right in your living room, if you will stop for your friend who is triggered by trauma and help them heal.

It is miraculous what Jesus wants to do for His children who are bound by trauma. He wants to give them part of their heavenly inheritance by offering them freedom in this life. Will you allow yourself to be utilized by the Holy Spirit in this way? Will you allow yourself to be a miracle worker even without the glory, the stardom, and the fanfare? Right now, in this moment, the Lord is asking you that question. "Son, Daughter, will you let Me move through your life in this way? Will you partner with Me to rescue My children from darkness? Will you let Me do miracles through you? Aren't you hungry to see My light and My love increase in this dark world? Partner with ME!"

CHAPTER FOURTEEN

PTKW

On the other side of each healing encounter with the Holy Spirit, we need to lay hold of **Post Traumatic Kingdom Wisdom**. Post-traumatic kingdom wisdom is the daily renewal of the mind after walking out of a triggered state into a place of deliverance. The assignment is to take what you have learned and meditate on the truth daily.

If what you gathered from an encounter with the Holy Spirit is that you needed to believe that you are worthy of love, then that truth now becomes what you strengthen yourself with on a daily basis, whether you are being challenged or not. Remind yourself, as you continue to heal, that you are worthy of being loved. Say out loud, "Thank you, Jesus, that You love me and that You declare me to be worthy of Your love." This is what renewing your mind with truth looks like. Saying it out loud involves more of your senses. The more senses you can employ in activating your new education, the more beneficial it will be to your brain.

Also, you can meditate on your new memories with Jesus. In every circumstance that follows, when the Enemy might try to bring up an echo or poke at that old place of pain, you will be able to grab onto your new understanding. The vulture, the Enemy, will come and try to steal your newfound freedom with his lies and deceit. Meditating on the truth you have gleaned will help you to stand against his tactics.

"Those along the path are the ones who hear, and then the devil comes and takes away the word from their hearts, so that they may not believe and be saved" (Luke 8:12 NIV).

The journey of resilience is built as you lean on the Holy Spirit as the Comforter. When you no longer seek places of refuge in your flesh, including dissociating or staying in a heightened arousal state, resilience increases in your life. The next time you are faced with something that has the potential to cause a trigger, it doesn't hit the mark in the same way. It becomes easier to navigate. The hardest part is the first time you face what would have caused a trigger in the past. It gets easier and easier after that. Why? It's because you have established a bonded history with God. You are building a history with Him. In moments that are scary or threaten fear, you can remind yourself of your history with Him. When you face a challenge, navigate it successfully, and then do it again and again, you are building resiliency. You are appropriating the Word of God when you take advantage of every triggered moment and respond by using it as a stepping stone toward Jesus. Reaching out to God for wisdom literally renews your mind and helps to pull all of the trauma out of your brain.

This also means you can no longer seek comfort elsewhere. Ask the Holy Spirit to reveal to you any area where you have sought comfort through something else. It could be vegging television all day long, eating a container of ice cream, shopping online all night, etc. Get real with God. Get transparent with the Holy Spirit. Ask Him to show you the places where you have pacified yourself with forms of comfort that weren't from Him. Be willing to give up any vice, any place, and anything that took His place of comfort in your life. It all has to be laid down so He can come all the way in.

This includes dissociating. You have to break agreement with the idea that dissociating is okay. It may have been a tool that kept you alive for a season, but you are not in that season anymore. There is responsibility when you receive revelation. Once you have the revelation, you are accountable for what you now know. Revelation isn't really revelation unless you do something with it. We need to put our newly gathered revelation into action by evaluating how we react to stressors in our life. We can take what we have learned and shift the reactions of our flesh. We can cast out demons, and be delivered from trauma, but we can't cast off our flesh. We have to crucify our flesh if we want to heal fully. We want our body, our flesh, and our habits to come into alignment with wholeness so our spirit can be unleashed and unbridled. We want to be able to take our intended position in the army of God. Being healed is part of being fully equipped to walk in our spirit into our full assignment in this life.

There is a prayer we love to pray in alignment with our faith as we walk out our healing, asking that we would be fully alive and in alignment with who God says He is. We pray, "Holy Spirit, let all seven fires of Your Spirit burn alive and active in me. Please fill me with the Spirit of Prophecy, the Spirit of Wisdom, the Spirit of Understanding, the Spirit of Counsel, the Spirit of Might, the Spirit of Knowledge, and the Spirit of the Fear of the Lord so that I will actively burn in all seven fires of Your Spirit, God. Lacking nothing, let me be fully equipped. Amen!"

"The Spirit of the Lord will rest on him— the Spirit of wisdom and of understanding, the Spirit of counsel and of might, the Spirit of the knowledge and fear of the Lord—and he will delight in the fear of the Lord" (Isaiah 11: 2-3 NIV).

The last action point we want to mention in Post Traumatic Kingdom Wisdom is to be in community. Trauma happens in isolation. In the midst of having trauma and even healing from trauma, you might have a tendency to want to isolate yourself and stay in a place of hiddenness. Please understand that part of healing is coming out of hiding and out of the habits of trauma-related behaviors. Hiding provides the Enemy with an opportunity to try to come back in and cause torment, so you want to come out of the lonely places where you have learned to feel comfortable. Step out, and find your people. Find a community of like-minded people. They are out there for you. You don't have to journey alone. Find a beautiful body of believers. Community heals. The Body of Christ is a community of people who are worthy of your friendship. Not everything is intended to be done alone. We need a community of healthy believers.

Anyone who has had trauma can gain so much healing by engaging with a community of healthy believers. Community is more powerful than the best therapists on the planet. Healthy, spirit-filled, loving, passionate followers of

Christ can demonstrate for you the very elements of development that you may not have received as a child.

Even if you tried to find community in the past, and ended up feeling hurt, you have to be willing to forgive and try again. We need each other. We need spiritual family in order to walk into the fullness of our healing and into the fullness of our identity in Christ. We can trust the Holy Spirit to lead us to a healthy body of believers who can help us grow stronger in our souls, minds, bodies, and spirits. Communicating, relating, and having friendships are all healing functions in the body of Christ. Like a skin graft, where the body heals the body, the Body of Christ heals the body.

The Holy Spirit can meet your needs, fill your heart, and heal your mind. He is the source of all true healing. He is completely competent to heal you all on His own, but He still loves to work through the body of Christ. The Kingdom of God is a family, not a corporation. We are meant to do life in a family, including the family of God. The Trinity is a family, and if God needs a family, so do you. Find your people.

CHAPTER FIFTEEN

PERSPECTIVE

One of the things we get asked about quite frequently is dissociative identity disorder (DID). The medical community classifies someone with DID as having multiple, distinct, different personalities. These personalities can be said to control a person's behavior and cause memory loss or delusions. I (Rachel) spent a good amount of time researching and studying this topic when I was in my master's degree program and in my Ph.D. program because of the complexity of the pain I witnessed in people who believed they were living with this diagnosis. It is a very sensitive topic, and we don't have the margin, nor do we sense the assignment, to fully address DID in the context of this material.

There is a hunger in people who feel lost and disillusioned as they try to make sense of their own situations related to severe trauma. The faith community isn't speaking to this tender issue very well, which can leave people feeling alone and without direction. That part is not okay with us. We can absolutely tell you that we are not medical professionals. We are not doctors. We are not claiming to be experts. We are not competing in this space to be considered a voice of authority on this topic for the general public. We are not offering medical advice. What we can offer you; however, is a general understanding of what we have witnessed in ministering to people with severe trauma.

Some traumatic experiences are so overwhelming, so devastating, and so intense that the person's mind dissociates into a fractured or protected part of their brain, storing within it the memory of the trauma being experienced. It is as if their brain detaches this experience and sets it aside because it is too painful to endure in the person's consciousness. This is also the part where demons seek to attach and where trauma memories are stored in the body.

Later in life, they may become aware that this fractured part of their heart and mind needs healing. It feels separate but alive in its own context. There are still emotions that are active within the fracture as well as nervous system memories alive within the fracture. It can almost feel like there is another little personality living within the person's brain. Mostly it feels like it is in the distance, but sometimes it can come closer to the surface when it is triggered.

For those who may have wondered if they have DID or have been diagnosed with it, but are unable to find a solution or healing, we would like to propose an optional way of understanding what might be a component. What some people explain as "multiple personalities," we would like to suggest may be a combination of fractured parts of their soul, at potentially varying ages, that are being triggered and pulled up into the consciousness of the right now, and possibly demons that have attached to those places of trauma.

Even though it is complex, logic helps us understand the possibility of a person's soul being wounded, and in a state of unresolved pain, that eventually makes itself known while still sounding and acting like it is stuck in the age of the initial trauma. It is plausible and explainable, even though it is complicated to wrap our understanding around. Where we struggle with the idea of DID is when it wants to normalize the concept of a forty-five-year-old man named Ralph, with a drinking and anger problem, as being a "part" of a twenty-five-year-old traumatized woman. A soul fracture from any traumatized age can be healed and made whole in Jesus. A different gender or personality manifesting in sin patterns is a demon trying to hide in the person's pain.

We have to be able to help people with this. We cannot allow wounded people to be exploited by the Enemy and kept in bondage. The medical community doesn't have the ability to help resolve this with counseling. You can't counsel a demon. The Holy Spirit is the Great Physician, and He has the solution for the wounded soul. No matter how traumatized the person may have been, God can redeem them and heal them. There is nothing too complicated for Jesus.

In very tender moments, we have sat with grown men and women, looking into their eyes and communicating with the childhood parts of their souls, watching Jesus lead them out of the places they have been trapped in. We have witnessed God bring healing, wholeness, oneness, integration, and freedom to so many fractured places in severely traumatized people's hearts. He is the solution for all things.

One person who asked us to share her story had an entire year of encounter after encounter with God, as He brought peace to her pieces. She had no idea that she had been dissociating for most of her life until she encountered the presence of the Lord so strongly that trauma began to surface. The Holy Spirit's love and presence were so strong and tangible that trauma quite literally began to shake out of her body. For several hours, during that first encounter, trauma shook out of her body while people were praying over her, and it was months later before she became aware that she even had fractured parts of her soul. She was in a ministry setting with a mentor who was praying over her, and suddenly an eleven-year-old little girl began to come up and speak out. This was the first of many encounters that she experienced over the months that followed.

This woman followed the Holy Spirit into the unknown by allowing Him to lead her into places of healing and deliverance. It took courage for her not to feel crazy and to yield to the leading of the Comforter while different parts of her fractured soul surfaced, cried, mourned, expressed their pain, told their story, and took Jesus by the hand, following Him as He put them to rest. Not once did a part of her soul that had been put to rest resurface again. Every demon that was hiding behind her trauma was removed. Every place of trauma lifted, and her soul was made whole. Every fractured part bonded with God and allowed Him to exchange her pain for His peace.

We follow Jesus's lead, and he has led us to precious little hearts who needed to walk down a path of rescue. We are awed by the precision of His knowledge, understanding, and patience with each precious piece of every courageous heart who journeys with Him into the healing of trauma.

He cradles His lambs in His arms throughout the timeline of their lives until they are fully one with Him. He stays by their side as they join Him in becoming complete and whole, unified with Him in mind, heart, and soul. To witness and participate in such a miraculous transformation establishes precedence that what Jesus does for one little heart, He will do for every little heart. There is no pain so deep, no place so dark, no trauma so tormenting that it removes you from the reach of God. He will always rescue His little lambs. Always.

As we close out our time together in this final chapter, we really want to commend you. Whether you are using this material in order to press into healing for yourself, or you are seeking to be a support to others, you have been equipped by Heaven's strategies. These methods were imparted to us by the Holy Spirit, and we want to share them with anyone who has a heart to receive them. We have personally seen how effective and liberating they can be.

We want to caution you as you move forward. Don't approach this work as a means of looking for a platform. Instead, look for the entrance in the servant's quarters. Look in the trenches and in the places that seem easier to avoid. Search for the places of pain in people's lives that others may tend to snub or look away from because they seem too difficult. Don't be intimidated; be in faith.

"Bear one another's burdens, and so fulfill the law of Christ" (Gal 6:2). The law of Christ is the law of love and liberty.

Also, be encouraged by Galatians 6:9-10. *"And let us not grow weary, while doing good, for in due season, we shall reap if we do not lose heart. Therefore, as we have the opportunity, let us do good to all, especially to those who are of the household of faith."*

We want to remind you again that this ministry requires patience. Partnering with someone through their trauma may not be a one-and-done situation. Oftentimes, people need several encounters with the Holy Spirit to heal from trauma. You may need to have multiple meetings or phone calls with an individual as they reach out to you in the midst of a trigger. How many times it takes is irrelevant. When you say "yes" to walking with someone through trauma, your heart needs to be in it until they cross the finish line. That is what Jesus did for us. He crossed the finish line and won our victory with His last breath. We need to be willing to do the same. This includes being patient with ourselves. We need to be forbearing with ourselves until we cross the finish line into our victory as well.

Imagine walking into a room with a hundred babies in cribs. All of them are crying at the top of their lungs. All of them are hurting, and all of them need attention. There is a constant orchestra of screams and torment. That is what trauma feels and sounds like on the inside of a person's body, and that person is one caregiver. Would you go into a room with a hundred-plus screaming infants and holler out, "BE QUIET!"? How many times do you think that person tried to do that already? How often did they try to silence the cries in their soul? How many times did they try and fail? The reality is that each wounded place, each broken piece, has to be attended to by the Comforter. One at a time. One at a time. One at a time. Each piece represents a part of their worldview that wasn't properly formed because of an experience that was extremely painful. Each part of them has to be comforted, one piece at a time.

If you are the person who says "yes" to walking with another through the healing process, you are being trusted by God to help that person be at rest and be at peace. You have to see yourself the way God sees you. If you are being chosen by someone to walk with them, that is not just them choosing you; that is God choosing you. They are being led by their spirit, so own that. God is entrusting you with a person's heart. He is trusting you to be an ambassador of His love. That is an overwhelmingly humbling place to walk in. You may feel very inadequate, but know that God is choosing you, and He can move through you. He can do it. Be encouraged that you can do all things through Christ; He will strengthen you. You can walk with someone as God fills the gaps in their heart and ministers to all the places where they weren't loved well in their life. You can walk out this assignment. Remember to be patient.

We want to close by encouraging you with this truth. Finding rest for your soul IS holy closure. His peace IS the answer to our wounded pieces. It is His peace.

"Come to me all you who are weary and burdened and I will give you rest, take My yoke upon you and learn from me, for I am gentle and humble in heart, and you will find rest for your souls. For My yoke is easy, and My burden is light" (Matthew 11: 28 NIV). You don't have to stay exhausted. He has rest for your soul.

He has peace for the parts of your heart that are crying still. You have permission to be healed. **You** are the beloved of God. You are His son. You are His daughter. You are precious to Him, and He is coming into the room where the babies are crying. He is bringing healing. You don't have to muster up a sense of worthiness. You just simply yield and surrender. You just have to let Him. He already wants to do it. He already paid the price to do it, and He has already established your victory. He is just asking, "Can I have this? Can I heal it? Baby girl or boy, your heart is hurting. Can I take the pain? I am here for you to be free; will you let Me help you? Will you engage your faith?"

Don't tell yourself to suck it up and move on. Don't look at the people around you and think, "Well, my life is not as bad as theirs; I need to get over myself." How many times do we say these things to ourselves? There is more for you. You have permission to heal. You are not reading this by mistake.

He knows every place, every moment, every second of your life, and every hair on your head. He also knows everything that happened to you, big and small, as well as everything that didn't happen to you but should have. He knows it all (Psalm 139).

You have His permission to heal. You have permission to ask Him, "Lord, give me a vision of how You see me. What is my life going to look like in heaven? Who will I be when I am completely free? How much of that can I have right now? I want it, Lord. I don't want to limp through the rest of my life. Set me ablaze! Set me on fire for You, God. Help me to yield as You heal my heart, and help me to partner with You as You heal others. I want to make an impact for Your Kingdom." God invites us to meditate on our kingdom identity. It's a healthy activity to imagine who you are in eternity. Meditating on God and His promises over our lives keeps us in peace.

"You will keep him in perfect peace, Whose mind is stayed on You, Because he trusts in You" (Isaiah 26:3).

It is hard to make an impact for the Kingdom of God if you are unwilling to heal. It is different if you are healing as you go, and you have permission to heal as you go. But **we** have to be willing to heal if we are encouraging others to heal as well. Again, you have permission to heal. We are asking you to increase your faith for healing.

You are needed! The Kingdom of God needs you to be whole, healed, set free, liberated, deployed, set on fire, rescuing others, and walking in the power of the Holy Ghost. This is why you are here. You were born to be loved, and you were born to radically love with every ounce of your being, every moment for the rest of your life. Loving God and loving other people is the reason you are alive.

Beloved, you are so deeply loved.

Dear Heavenly Father, bless our friends with Your undeniable presence. We pray that every cry of their heart will be rocked in the cradle of Your arms. We declare wholeness of mind, soul, and body. Pour the oil of Your healing comfort over every brain that has endured trauma. We speak holy closure to every memory. Reveal Your beauty, Jesus, as You shine Your light of truth into every desperate place. Encounter them so profoundly that they always remember your rescue. Close every door of suffering with Your fiery love. Every onslaught against them be abolished by Your authority.

Father, You are faithful to keep what is committed to You, and You finish everything You start. We declare every need met, every cry heard, and every weakness strengthened, in Your name.

Thank You, Jesus, for using this season of healing to equip and launch our beloved friends into their kingdom purposes. We declare that no weapon formed against them will prosper in each community they are meant to join and every assignment they are given. We declare full redemption to their history as You use them mightily to set the captives free. Everything the locusts have eaten and the fire has scorched must be made new again within them and everyone else within their sphere of influence. We call forth all those You have predestined for them to impact with their testimony and newfound education. Prepare the way for them to be used for Your glory. Remove every obstacle that would stand in their way. We prophesy supernatural maturation for every seed sown through this book of healing and understanding, *Peace to the Pieces*.

May peace and rest follow their lives from this day forward. May our friends never stop drinking from the refreshing wellspring of The Holy Spirit. We pray their relationship with You grows exponentially. We decree that the love of God through their lives will torment the devil and all his horde of influencers. May every demon choke on their peace. We declare healing and restoration for all of eternity. We prophesy that their hunger for more of You will never cease. Let it be written so in the archives of Heaven. In the mighty name of our beloved Jesus Christ, Amen.

AFTERWORD

I (Rachel) want to share a little bit about the journey I have been on with the Holy Spirit as He has taught me how to understand trauma and healing. I went to school for counseling for many years. I earned a bachelor's degree in pastoral counseling and a master's degree in counseling. I was a few classes and one dissertation away from my Ph.D. in counseling, and the Lord asked me to lay it all down and follow Him into this education instead.

I had worked hard for so many years, trying to learn and glean how to really help people overcome. I longed to see real freedom for people who are bound in pain. Through my education, I learned so much about why things happen, why people do the things they do, how our brains are wired, our relational tendencies, and how as humans, we get so bound. What I often found lacking, however, was the solution for how to recover and heal from those places. I gained so much compassion and so much understanding, but while all of my classes and research offered coping methods they always seemed lacking in the hope of healing, or the steps to actual freedom. I often cried out to the Lord for more. I wanted more understanding, more wisdom, and more of His insight into the hearts of His children. *"In all your getting, get understanding"* (Proverbs 4:7). This Scripture is our standard and the reason why we keep pressing in for more.

The understanding we have been sharing in this book is part of where He led me. I walked away from the titles and letters at the end of my name that offered me some kind of credibility for the things I was saying. I am not communicating that education is wrong. It can be a wonderful tool. But on this subject, I took God's hands and let His Spirit lead the way through. He gets all of the credit. He does the work. He works the miracles. What a relief to not have to have all of the answers. I traded my books for a midwife's basin and towel and have seen Him move in incomprehensible ways. His Spirit will lead us to an even higher education if we allow Him.

I (Rachel) would also like to take a moment to honor my co-author, Amber, who is my aunt and friend. Amber also has an incredible, decades-long backstory of being educated by the Holy Spirit, while watching God lead people into miraculous healing. The Holy Spirit kept her set apart and protected her education. He pulled her very close in His desire to be her primary place of learning. She has followed Him down many faith-filled pathways as she ministers to His wounded lambs. Her prophetic insight and precision of discernment create such an atmosphere of love and healing. So many people have been healed and set free through the ministry of her life. I have never once seen her reach for accolades or need acknowledgment. She loves with the purest, most selfless love and washes people's feet, in the spirit, as they heal and break free from bondages. She does this mostly in quiet, unassuming places where there are no big crowds paying witness or being audience to her sacrifices. She is a treasure from heaven, and her life is poured out in these pages.

I (Amber) have been on my own adventure with the Holy Spirit since I was a child. In God's kindness, He encountered me in supernatural ways from a very young age and purposefully educated me in the understanding of how Kingdom healing operates. For the last few decades, and through the leading of the Holy Spirit, I have been gifted the opportunity to prophetically walk with anyone God puts in my life. I have had a front-row seat as God moves in the hearts of His precious children and restores all the places within them that the Enemy tried to harm.

I (Amber) cannot put the last period on this book without first honoring Rachel, my sweet niece, and her walk with the Lord. I have witnessed firsthand the depth of spiritual knowledge Rachel moves in. She's much richer and fuller having trusted God for His wisdom. Her connection to

God's heart for his people is breathtaking. If you've ever had the opportunity to hear her teach, you'll know just how anointed she is to communicate freedom for an entire room. If you ever need to dive into God's love, go find Rachel and get a hug. Trust me on this, you'll never be the same again. We have testimonies to back it up. She is talented on so many levels. She has a bucket with everybody's name on it in her heart. Rachel is all about seeds: collecting them, planting them, watering them, and giving away the harvest.

Thank you, Dear Friends, for being courageous enough to pick up this book and allow the Holy Spirit to walk you into deeper places of healing. As you keep pressing in for more of Jesus, expect Him to use your story of healing as a catalyst for others to find their own place of victory.

Remember, trauma doesn't get the last word. As soon as we make room for the Holy Spirit, He comes into our mess and brings His perfect peace to all of our pieces.

Made in United States
Troutdale, OR
10/18/2023

13761720R00080